**Dedicated to Bapuji,
his 5th grandson Arun M. Gandhi,
Arun's late wife Sunanda Gandhi,
and their son Tushar A. Gandhi**

GANDHI'S NAMES
Mohandas Karamchand Gandhi
Mahatma Gandhi
Father of the Nation
Bapu or Bapuji
('Ji' at the end of one's name signifies respect)

Mohandas K. Gandhi
October 2, 1869 to January 30, 1948

FAMILY NAMING
Mohandas Karamchand Gandhi
Manilal Mohandas Gandhi (second son)
Arun Manilal Gandhi (grandson)
Tushar Arun Gandhi (great-grandson)

A Life-Changing Journey Through
the Heart of Gandhi's India

Las Vegas, Nevada

Gandhi Legacy Tour of India 'The Book'
Published by Catalyst House
a DBA imprint of ADMAX, LLC

Founded: April 17, 2002
Las Vegas, Nevada

©2022 Lynnea Bylund
First Printing January 2022

All rights reserved. No part of this book, in part or in whole, may be reproduced, transmitted, or utilized in any form or by any means, electronic, photographic, or mechanical, including photocopying, recording, or by any information storage and retrieval system without permission in writing from Catalyst House, except for quotations and reviews.

Publisher site: www.CatalystHouse.net
North Las Vegas, Nevada
Comments and inquiries: publisher@catalysthouse.com

ISBN: 979-8-9855271-1-7

Book & Cover Design/Edit by Marcus Dalton & Lynnea Bylund
Title Logo design by Tom Ross / www.tomross.com
Set in Helvetica, Abadi & Comic Sans MS
Final Copy Edit by Arun Gandhi

Gandhi Legacy Tour of India 2009-2018 – visit www.GandhiTour.info/India

NOTE FROM THE PUBLISHER

As a publisher, Catalyst House embraces the principles of a Global Cooperative Forum – a new paradigm for world relations and economy based on the tenets of Not-Two Is Peace by Adi Da, which presumes the "prior unity" underlying all of humanity. With each new book, the Catalyst House publishing mission addresses a broad array of challenges to human and earth-kind in the increasingly tumultuous 21st century. Given that we are all literally in the same boat, possessing the technological means to destroy the planet, Catalyst House publishes books to inspire a transformative consciousness that is urgently required; one that informs and inspires collective constructive action embraceable by all. Gandhi's living realpolitik of 'Ahimsa' (non-violence), and the recognition of the prior unity common to us all, IS the publishing mission and urgency that we embrace.

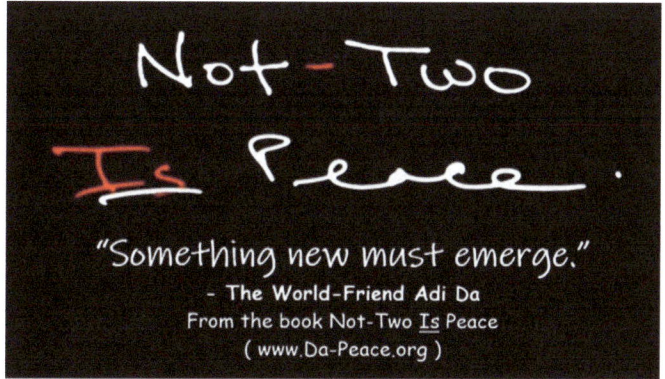

**The World-Friend Adi Da
from Not-Two Is Peace
(www.Da-Peace.org)**

Mission Catalyst! – cat*a*lyst (kat'l-ist) n.

1. That which instigates sudden acceleration of forces!
2. Something that causes important events to happen!
3. An agent who provokes significant change or action!

The mission of Catalyst House is to facilitate extraordinary change and acceleration for its portfolio of authors, projects, and initiatives: fomenting new publishing channels, venues, ventures, and philanthropic influence. Emphasizing emerging trends, natural health and sustainable enterprise, Catalyst House provides its author-clients with publishing, product and service alliances across a panoply of interests and urgencies.

Sales of Gandhi Legacy Tour of India "The Book"
benefit inner-city school children.

The toil of the Kolhapur Brickyards | Scott Kafora

SPECIAL ACKNOWLEDGEMENTS

Foremost, we acknowledge the Divine in each of us. Namaste!

We acknowledge Mohandas K. Gandhi, the Mahatma venerated by a nation as 'Bapuji' (India's Great Father), for his life's demonstration of "transcendental activism" - transcending and going beyond oneself in order to make real change in the world.

Our heartfelt gratitude goes out to our mentor and Gandhi Legacy Tour founder/leader, Arun Gandhi, for his dedication to sharing his grandfather's personal and intimate lessons of love and the path of nonviolence in the world. In addition, for his one-pointed commitment to actively "Be the change we wish to see in the world."

Arun practices wisdom, learned directly from his grandfather, with his children and they in turn live it with theirs. As an example, Arun would beg his grandfather for an autograph he felt he deserved and never received. In all of Arun's badgering of his grandfather for the autograph including total disruptions of important political meetings with Nehru and others, Gandhi never lost his patience with his unruly grandson, he responded in love by gently drawing Arun's head to his heart as he continued talking politics.

Observing Gandhi family interactions over the past decade it becomes readily apparent that Gandhi's examples, of kind love and mutual respect truly lived, unites them. They are each other's grandest supporters, which provides a foundation for love to grow and ensures positive impact for future generations to come.

Bapuji did an amazing job in not only transforming politics and activism around the world, he also did an amazing job in transforming himself as a man.

FURTHER ACKNOWLEDGMENTS ARE IN ORDER FOR...

- Sunanda Gandhi, Arun's late wife and tour co-founder, and Tushar Gandhi, Arun's son and Legacy Tour co-leader.
- The India 'on the ground' guidance of Alok Tiwari and his Travel Passion Agency team for making it always a safe and meaningful lifelong experience for everyone.
- Scott Kafora, for his support of AVANI while residing full time in Kolhapur, India since early 2010.
- Images noted throughout this fine work were provided by, and we owe a great debt of thanks to, Kasturi Gandhi, Scott Kafora, Nipun Prabhakar, Mathew Rhoades and Mat Fuller.
- And it must also be said, a big thanks to the Gandhi Worldwide Education Institute; Kit Miller and the MK Gandhi Institute of Nonviolence; Salisbury University; and Rollins College for their consistent support and passionate participation.
- And finally, our deepest gratitude to all who have embarked on this special journey. Gandhi Legacy Tour of India has led nearly 300 **people** along this life-changing journey since inception; and to all of you, we salute you in 'prior unity' and satyagraha!

"Whatever you do will be insignificant, but it is very important that you do it." – Gandhi

GANDHI'S TIMELINE

INDIA
- 1869, October 2, Gandhi was Born in the coastal town of Porbandar
- 1876, Gandhi began primary school in Rajkot
- 1881, Gandhi entered high school in Rajkot
- 1883, May, at age 13 Gandhi married Kasturba in an arranged marriage
- 1884, Gandhi entered a rebellious adolescent phase
- 1885, Gandhi's father, Karamchand, died at 63 years old

LONDON
- 1888, September 4, Gandhi traveled to London to train as a barrister
- 1892, June 12, Gandhi returns to India from London after passing the Bar

SOUTH AFRICA
- 1893, April 13, Gandhi traveled to South Africa to work for Indian conglomerate DaDa Abdulla & Co
- 1893, May 24, Gandhi first arrived in Durban, South Africa
- 1893, June 7, Gandhi is famously ejected from a South Africa train in Pietermaritzburg
- 1894, August 22, Gandhi founds the natal India Congress
- 1897, January 10, Gandhi is attacked by white settlers in Durban upon returning from India
- 1899, October 17, Gandhi Organized the Indian Ambulance Corps during the 2nd Boer War
- 1904, November, Gandhi founded the Phoenix Settlement in Durban; he moves there June 2, 1906
- 1906, September 11, Gandhi Introduced the Satyagraha philosophy of nonviolent protest
- 1908, January 10, Gandhi is arrested for the first time for refusing to carry an ID card
- 1908-1909 Gandhi lived at the Satyagraha House commonly known as the Gandhi House
- 1910, May 30, Gandhi established Tolstoy Farm
- 1913, November 6, Gandhi led the 'Great March' to gain India Rights
- 1914, June 27, Gandhi met with South Africa's highest ranking officer Field Marshal Jan Smuts
- 1914, June, Gandhi suspended the South African Struggle after winning passage of the Indian Relief Act
- 1914, July 8, Gandhi was presented with addresses at a farewell townhall gathering in Durban
- 1914, July 11, Gandhi leaves his Phoenix Settlement for the last time
- 1914, July 15, Gandhi recognizes fallen resistance leaders Valliamma & Naggappen at Bloemfontein Cemetery
- 1914, July 18, Gandhi arrives Cape Town via procession, bids permanent farewell to South Africa and boards the S.S. Kinfauna Castle bound for England, after which he would return to India

RETURN TO INDIA
- 1915, January 9, Gandhi received a hero's welcome upon returning to India from South Africa via England
- 1917, April, Gandhi traveled to Champaran to investigate conditions of local farmers
- 1917, June 17, Gandhi established Sabarmati Ashram
- 1918, January, Gandhi advocated on behalf of farmers in Kheda subject to extreme taxation during a famine
- 1919, March, British government passed the Rowlatt Act indefinitely extending the use of emergency measures
- 1919, April 13, Jallianwala Bagh Massacre
- 1920, September, Gandhi launched the non-violence/non-cooperation movement
- 1921, Gandhi resolved to wear only loincloth promoting khadi, mass civil resistance follows, 1000s jailed
- 1921, December, Gandhi is given exclusive authority over the Indian National Congress
- 1922, March 10, Gandhi is arrested on charges of inciting violence
- 1924, February 5, Gandhi is released from prison after two years of a six-year sentence, following surgery
- 1924, September 18, Gandhi began a 21 day fast to attempt reconciliation of Hindus and Muslims
- 1925, September, Gandhi founded the All-India Spinners association
- 1927, Gandhi's "The Story of My Experiments with Truth" is published
- 1929, Gandhi was arrested for burning foreign cloth in Calcutta
- 1930, January 26, Purna Swaraj, India's Declaration of Independence, is decreed by India National Congress
- 1930, March 12, Gandhi embarked on the Salt March Protest
- 1930, April 6, Gandhi arrived in Dandi, Gujarat, finishing the Salt March and publicly breaking the Salt Law
- 1930, May 4, Gandhi is arrested and imprisoned
- 1931, January 26, Gandhi is released
- 1932, January 4, Gandhi is arrested
- 1932, September, Gandhi while in prison began a 6 day fast to protest separate elections for untouchables
- 1933, February 11, Gandhi began the weekly 'Harijan' to champion rights of 'Dalits' (the untouchables)
- 1933, November 7, Gandhi began a ten-month tour of India to end untouchability
- 1934, India National Congress passed the "Quit India" resolution, the final national Satyagraha campaign
- 1934, September 17, Gandhi announced his retirement from politics to focus on village economics
- 1936, April 30, Gandhi relocated his base of operations to Sevagram Ashram
- 1942, August 9, Gandhi is arrested and imprisoned at Aga Khan Palace
- 1942, February 22, Gandhi's wife Kasturba dies at Aga Khan Palace, she was 74
- 1946, August 25, Gandhi Leaves Sevagram Ashram, his residence of a decade
- 1947, August 15, India is partitioned and granted independence
- 1948, January 12, Gandhi undertook a five-day fast to end Hindu and Muslim violence in Delhi.
- 1948, January 30, 5:05 p.m., Having survived five previous attempts during his final 14 years, Gandhi was assassinated; His last words were: "Ram Ram Ram" (God God God)

An enterprising produce vendor greets us with a smile in Old Ahmedabad | Mat Fuller

CONTENTS

- NOTE FROM THE PUBLISHER v
- SPECIAL ACKNOWLEDGEMENTS viii
- GANDHI'S TIMELINE ix
- PREFACE 1
- FOREWORD by Arun Gandhi 3
- INTRODUCTION by Lynnea Bylund 5
- CHHATRAPATI SHIVAJI AIRPORT 9
- MUMBAI - MANI BHAVAN 11
- A WORD ABOUT KUMKUM 13
- MUMBAI - WOMEN'S INDIA TRUST 15
- KOLHAPUR – AVANI 17
- A STORY OF RESCUE 19
- PUNE - AGA KHAN PALACE 21
- MUMBAI - MARKETPLACE|SHARE 25
- GANDHI & TRAIN TRAVEL 27
- TRAVELING THROUGH THE KUTCH by Kasturi Gandhi 29
- HUNNARSHALA FOUNDATION 33
- KHAMIR RESOURCE CENTER 35
- SALT BEDS OF KUTCH 37
- AHMEDABAD - GUJARAT VIDYAPITH 41
- SABARMATI ASHRAM 43
- AHMEDABAD – S.E.W.A. 49
- THE S.E.W.A. SUCCESS by Dr. Margaret McLaren 51
- OLD AHMEDABAD HERITAGE WALK 53
- TILONIA AJMER - BAREFOOT COLLEGE 57
- STORY OF SANJIT 'BUNKER' ROY 59
- WATERMAN OF INDIA 63
- TARUN BHARAT SANGH 65
- DEHRADUN – NAVDANYA 67
- NEW DEHLI - BIRLA HOUSE 71
- RAJ GHAT MEMORIAL 73
- DEHLI – THE QUTUB MINAR 77
- AGRA - TAJ MAHAL 79
- RED FORT OF AGRA 83
- INDIRA GANDHI INT'L 87
- EPILOGUE – GANDHI'S 'TALISMAN OF RECALL' 89
- IMAGE CREDITS 92
- MEET THE AUTHOR 107

"Peace is its own reward." - Gandhi

PREFACE

*"His was a challenging journey -
- and it changed the world."*

AVANI student, Kolhapur | Mat Fuller

He was a delicate and fragile man with glasses and a customary Hindu waistcloth, used a bamboo walking stick, and had a near-toothless smile. His outward appearance was that of a humble unassuming holy man; and fortified only with terrific bravery and an unshakeable dedication to nonviolent resistance Gandhi persevered and ultimately prevailed over one of history's greatest empires.

Twelve months subsequent to India's independence Gandhi was slain in 1948 in Delhi; but his impact continues to increase and its influence felt. As Nelson Mandela declared in 2007, "In a world driven by violence and strife, Gandhi's message of peace and non-violence holds the key to human survival in the 21st century."

Trek with us as we traverse Gandhi's path across India and meet the green shoots of his vision taking hold in a world crying out for change.

"We must be the change that we wish to see in the world." - Gandhi

Wise woman in Old Mumbai | Mat Fuller

Blessed by a child in Kolhapur | Scott Kafora

Teenagers in Ahmedabad | Mat Fuller

Spiritual Renunciates in Old Mumbai | Mat Fuller

FOREWORD by Arun Gandhi

Arun Gandhi 2017 | Scott Kafora

The Gandhi Legacy Tour does not focus on places of tourist interest, but rather places of human interest. It is designed to educate in the essence of my grandfather's philosophy of nonviolence and how individuals may apply it to bring about socio-economic change.

Gandhi believed in creating a "Sarvodaya" society — where everyone would enjoy a reasonably good standard of living with attendant rights and privileges. This can be created simply by compassionate citizens constructively helping the less fortunate improve their circumstance.

Gandhi's philosophy of nonviolence is like that of the iceberg – what is visible to the eye is only a fraction of what is hidden. "Nonviolence is a lifestyle that one must adopt." Scholars have analyzed over and over the part that deals with political conflicts and independence of nations, because they insist that nonviolence is simply a strategy of convenience; and my Grandfather has spoken to this:

"My philosophy is not like a jacket you wear when necessary and discard when not. Non-violence is a lifestyle that one must embrace, which means allowing love, respect, compassion, and acceptance to emerge and to dominate one's attitude. Then we build good relations, not only within the family but outside of the family. We will no longer be selfish and greedy but magnanimous and giving."

Grass roots action is obvious throughout Gandhi's India

It is no secret that official India abandoned Gandhi's philosophy upon gaining its independence from British rule in 1947; however, there are many at the grassroots level, young and old, who are still inspired by his philosophy and have put it into action to bring about quantitative and qualitative changes within the Indian society.

Many have started projects to bring solace to the poor of whom there are more than 500 million in India. The Gandhi Legacy Tour of India explores these wonderful projects in the cities and in the villages to see firsthand how people have used Gandhi's philosophy in everyday life.

Among the many diversities in India the one that divides the westernized urban India and the traditional rural India is the most odious. Urban India is not India at all and we shall explore this on the tour, while the traditional India, my grandfather's India, is the true heart of India. We are delighted to have you join us for a photo-journey tour of our Gandhi Legacy Adventure!

Arun Gandhi, founder M.K. Gandhi Institute for Nonviolence and Gandhi Worldwide Education Institute; author of 10 books including The Forgotten Woman (with Sunanda Gandhi) and The Gift of Anger

"As human beings, our greatness lies not so much in being able to remake the world – that is the myth of the atomic age – as in being able to remake ourselves." – Gandhi

> "One is ever young in the felt presence of the God of Truth, or Truth which is God." – Gandhi

AVANI student greets us with a Sign of 'Namaste' | Scott Kafora

INTRODUCTION
by Lynnea Bylund

My own Gandhian journey was empowered by good fortune when I was invited by Arun Gandhi, to join the 2009 Gandhi Legacy Tour, and soon after I was elected to Arun's non-profit organization Gandhi Worldwide Education Institute as a director and finance officer. For seven years, I also served as Managing Director for the Gandhi Legacy Tour company. This book is a resultant labor of love and gratitude.

Some context to Gandhi's revolution…

Prior to the Revolution of Mahatma Gandhi, culminating in India's return to independence in 1947, Indians had known British 'Raj' (rule) for nearly 200 years, at least since 1757 under England's flagship corporate entity, the East India Company; and after 1858 directly under the British flag.

In 1858 when direct British Raj took effect, Queen Victoria assured that the British government would endeavor to improve the standing and plight of its Indian subjects.

To the British, this meant schooling the Indians in British forms of thought and eradicating Indian culture in the process. The British also practiced "divide and rule" policies, pitting Hindus and Muslims against one another. Further, subsequent to the British Raj, Indians were prevented from holding political and public office in their own land.

After nearly a half century of valiant struggle, in August of 1947, India (and its Muslim offshoot, Pakistan) achieved independence under the leadership of 'Bapu' (the affectionate name by which most Indians referred to their "Father of Independent India"

The forefront of 'philanthropic tourism'

Recent decades have seen a substantial growth in philanthropic-based tourism: using travel to give back to those less fortunate. Still, in practice what often is confronted is that selecting a particular travel mission is quite daunting; philanthropic tour missions desiring to make a difference often don't know where or how to begin, or whether their efforts will really make a meaningful lasting impact. The United Nations Educational, Scientific and Cultural Organization (UNESCO) states that, "Travel Philanthropy is a natural interlocutor between the wealth and desires of the global traveler and the socio-economic needs of some of the world's most remote, but heritage-rich communities, natural and cultural sites."

As Nobel laureate Wangari Maathai observed in 2008: "Travel philanthropy was born out of the frustration with conventional aid and ineffective philanthropic giving, as a form of development assistance flowing from the travel industry and travelers directly into conservation initiatives, community projects and philanthropic organizations."

The concept of "doing good" by "giving back," while engaging in life-changing world travel, is an enticing proposal, but the reality is that we often fail to understand our true role as caring people visiting unfamiliar cultures.

The dedication of volunteer-abroad type programs, like Peace Corps, Raleigh International and Maximo Niveland, is admirable, but charitable tourism fills a unique and potentially much wider niche: helping those in need without requiring an extended commitment of time. Across the globe, philanthropic travelers increasingly provide monetary resources, time, and talent to further the wellbeing of less fortunate local and village communities. Within these pages are provided an intimate experience of unique philanthropic travel though parts of India and groups that remain closely associated with the impact and phenomena of Gandhi: in the past, at present, and most importantly, in the future.

~ Journey with us as we traverse through the heart of Gandhi's India and see his seeds taking sprout! ~

"There is something in us all that hungers after the good and true, and when we glimpse it in people, we applaud them for it. Through them we let the world's pain into our hearts, and we find compassion. When things go wrong or have been terribly wrong for some time, their inspiration reminds us of the tenderness for life that we can all feel." -Archbishop Desmond Tutu

Our journey begins …

"If India adopted the doctrine of love as an active part of her religion and introduced it in her politics, self-rule would descend upon India from heaven. But I am painfully aware that such an event remains far off as yet." – Gandhi

NOW ARRIVING …

CHHATRAPATI SHIVAJI AIRPORT

Our journey begins with the glare of 21st Century marvel - Chhatrapati Shivaji International is the primary international airport of Mumbai India. The Airport's IATA code – "BOM", is derived from Bombay, as Mumbai was previously known –and it is India's busiest airport in terms of passenger traffic, second only to Delhi's Indira Gandhi International Airport.

BOM is India's most modern international travel hub and were it not for the bustling mob of traditionally dressed travelers, this modern-sweeping aerodrome would offer little hint of the India land-journey that would soon commence.

Classic works of Indian art adorn
Chhatrapati Shivaji Airport passages | fig. 3

First stop, Mumbai and the Mani Bhavan …

GANDHI & MLK

In 1959 the American Quakers and Gandhi Nat'l Memorial together invited Martin Luther King Jr, to visit India. Traveling with his wife, Coretta-Scott, King met with many who had directly participated in India's struggle against British rule. A visit to Mani Bhavan, Gandhi's national HQ for over a decade and a half, was scheduled; and King was granted permission to stay in Gandhi's room alone for an evening.

After a night stay King said, "Now I feel spiritually empowered to lead my people in the American civil rights struggle ahead."

Mani Bhavan beckons | Fig. 4

> "Jesus Christ showed us the way and Mahatma Gandhi of India proved it can work." — M.L.K Jr.

MUMBAI - MANI BHAVAN

As described at the Mani Bhavan website, this modest two story home near downtown Mumbai has quite a tale to tell. Mani Bhavan served as Gandhi's Bombay residence and HQ from 1917 to 1934 as he evolved from regional agitator to world radical catalyst for change. Mani Bhavan is where Gandhi introduced satyagraha (non-violent resistance) as a new and effective strategy to fight oppression and injustice. Satyagraha imbues the dynamism of the Mahatma himself even while he led a nation.

The Mani Bhavan was the center of the Great Freedom Struggle, with many important meetings held, decisions made, and movements launched. It was here in 1917 that Gandhi first learned to spin cotton on a Charkha, a traditional spinning wheel.

The Mani Bhavan is now a museum dedicated to Gandhian history and philosophy and has a rarified saintly air about it. In 1955 Mani Bhavan was dedicated as a memorial to Gandhi and to the significant activities he initiated from there. Mani Bhavan is also recognized as a Research Institute, preparing students for degrees in 'Gandhian Thought' and 'Rural Development.'

A hall of history | Fig. 6

King in his office circa 1960, Bob Fitch | Fig. 5

'Mani Bhavan' means 'jeweled house' and Gandhi initiated the Non-Cooperation, Satyagraha, Swadeshi, Khadi and Khilafat movements from Mani Bhavan. Gandhi's association with charkha (spinning wheel) began in 1917 while at Mani Bhavan.

Enter, the Mani Bhavan | Fig. 8

Gandhi's private quarters | Fig. 7

Front entrance plaque to Mani Bhavan | Fig. 9

A WORD ABOUT KUMKUM

When arriving at our projects, women wearing saris often greet our group by placing a round dot (bindi) or line on our foreheads as a way to acknowledge the divine in all. The colored dots or stripes of 'kumkum' (or 'kumkuma') – a powder used for social and religious markings in India – is made from turmeric mixed with other ingredients to achieve different color effects.

Kumkum is a unique cultural and spiritual symbol, and a significant part of the identity of Indian women (and men) who adorn their foreheads with it, and married women also apply it to the parting of their hair as commitment to long-life and well-being of their husbands.

> The reason a 'bindi' (dot) of kumkum is applied to the forehead stems from an ancient spiritual belief that a person is divided into 7 vortices of consciousness called chakras, starting at the base of spine and ending at the top of the head. The 6th chakra is centered in the forehead and is believed to be a channel to the Divine.

The colors of India begin with Kumkum | Figs. 10, 11, 12

First stop – Mumbai and the Women's India Trust …

WOMEN'S INDIA TRUST
Established in 1968, WIT has remained women-centric, continuing to help less fortunate women secure a better future.

> *"Strength comes not from physical capacity; ... it emanates from an indomitable will."* -Gandhi

MUMBAI - WOMEN'S INDIA TRUST

Women's India Trust (WIT) is a charitable organization established in 1968, which began by training under-privileged and unskilled women in Mumbai to stitch sari petticoats. Since then, WIT has added numerous educational vocational training and has helped thousands of women develop skills and earn a regular income, changing their lives for the better.

WIT has remained women-centric and continues to help less fortunate women secure a better future. WIT remains dedicated to the original aims of its founder, Kamila Tyabji: helping women to help themselves; to encourage women from less privileged backgrounds to acquire new skills, to give them the self-confidence and self-esteem required to earn by their own industry and initiative; to enable them to carry the newly developed skill into a wider world and within the framework of WIT.

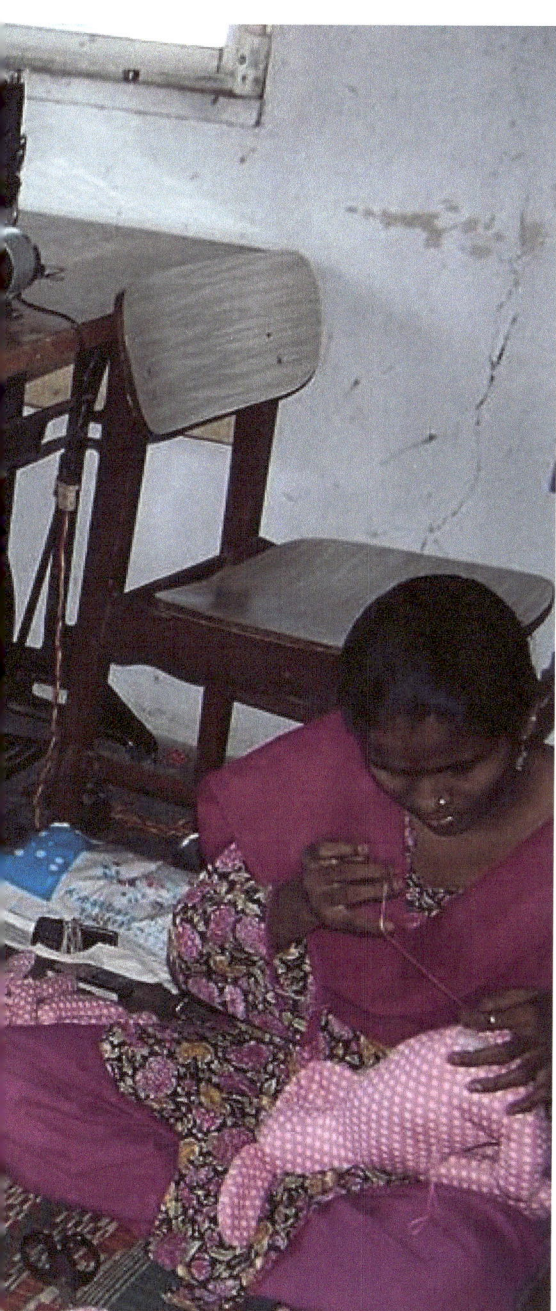

WIT artisans & staff, Mumbai | figs. 13 & 14

Next stop, Kolhapur & AVANI

AVANI Students, Arun Chavan (founder at right), Tushar & Arun Gandhi | fig. 15

Sunanda Gandhi dedication | fig. 16

AVANI Students | fig. 18

Mother & Child, labor camp, Kolhapur | fig. 17

*"If we are to teach real peace in this world...
... we shall have to begin with the children." - Gandhi*

KOLHAPUR – AVANI

AVANI is a small and extremely devoted team directed by Ms. Anuradha Bhosale, determined to wipe out child labor in the brickyard work sites in and around Kolhapur district of Maharashtra, India. The name AVANI is a conjunction of Marathi Indian language letters and words that convey 'food, clothing, and shelter.'

AVANI is led by Anuradha Bhosale, a regional activist-hero and renowned grassroots leader of women's rights and anti-child labor activism based in Kolhapur where more than 35,000 children are involved in daily labor for local industries. A former child-laborer herself at the age of six, Ms. Bhosale has spent decades fighting child exploitation, labor, trafficking, and female infanticide. AVANI coordinates the rescue efforts of children from work locations such as construction sites, domestic work, hotels and lodges.

AVANI's Ms. Anuradha Bhosale | figs. 19 & 20

The AVANI Residential Home also provides residence and care for children who have been rescued from work sites or vulnerable situations and now attend government schools. The AVANI Home provides food, residency, health and psychological support for these children. Many children are first generation learners.

AVANI school recess | fig. 21

Anuradha with student   fig. 22

CRC/Women of Kolhapur   fig. 23

Child Rights Campaign (CRC), a project of AVANI & Women of Kolhapur, concerns itself with the underprivileged sections of rural society. CRC-initiated action concentrates on championing of children's rights. "Safeguarding of children's rights is best done in an environment of overall progress of the weaker societal sectors," says Anuradha Bhosale

A STORY OF RESCUE
by Anuradha Bhosale

Since 1998, the AVANI organization has been championing child labor issues in Kolhapur, India. It is our sacred mission to identify and rescue child laborers from different industries and then rehabilitate them. To identify our child candidates, we conduct our own reconnaissance in the brickyard labor camps, the farms, hotels, restaurants, commercial and retail industries.

In 2003, while investigating a nearby village, we found several child laborers. Our social workers were shocked to find a girl just 5 years old working with her mother mixing soil and water together to make bricks. The mother of two had suffered abuse at the hands of her husband for many years before he finally abandoned the family altogether. She had no other means of living and had to move from her village to a brickyards labor camp.

Due to her extreme poverty, her 5-year-old daughter, Sonali also had to work to support the family. Sonali worked 8 hours a day, 7 days a week helping her mother by carrying bricks from one place to another for curing. Her minimum daily quota was to carry 1,000 bricks on her head for which she was paid 15 cents per day.

AVANI student, Sonali, at the head of the class | fig. 24

We were shocked at this, our first experience at witnessing such depths of child exploitation. We began counseling Sonali's mother and assured her that AVANI would take care of her food, clothes, shelter, health and education. Her mother was understandably suspicious, however, after she visited our small home for rescued child laborers and visited with the other children, her doubts were soon assuaged.

As Sonali progressed through her primary education, she developed natural leadership abilities and soon started looking out for all the other children. By the time she reached high school, she had matured nicely, developing good study habits, an appreciation for learning and a curiosity about what her future might be with the opportunity of going to college.

In 2017, Sonali was accepted at one of the top nursing colleges in a large metropolitan city several hours from Kolhapur. It should also be understood that all science classes in India are taught in English, which required her mastery. Sonali now sees that her hard work, even in learning a second language, is finally paying off. After completing college and becoming a nurse, Sonali plans to support her mother for the remainder of her life…

… **and it is for this mission that AVANI exists!**

On to Pune & Aga Khan Palace…

Aga Khan Palace | figs. 25 - 28

SOME MILESTONES IN MAHATAMAJI'S LIFE AT THE AGAKHAN PALACE

Gandhiji and his wife Kasturbaji were interned in this palace in 1942 after the declaration of the "Quit India Resolution". He was accompanied by Miraben, Shri. Pyarelal Nayar, Smt. Sarojini Naidu, Dr. Sushila Nayar and his Personal Secretary, Shri. Mahadevbhai Desai.

- 10 August 1942- Gandhiji and his colleagues were brought here from Bombay.
- 15 August 1942- Shri. Mahadevbhai Desai died of a heart attack.
- 26 January 1943 Gandhiji hoisted the congress flag at these premises.
- 19 March 1943- Smt. Sarojini Naidu was released because of ill health.
- 26 January 1944- Gandhiji hoisted the Congress flag at these premises.
- 22 February 1944- "Mahashivratri" Kasturba breathed her last after a prolonged illness.
- 06 May 1944- Gandhiji and his colleagues were released from Agakhan Palace.

"Aga Khan displayed infinite patience, understanding and wisdom." -Gandhi

PUNE - AGA KHAN PALACE

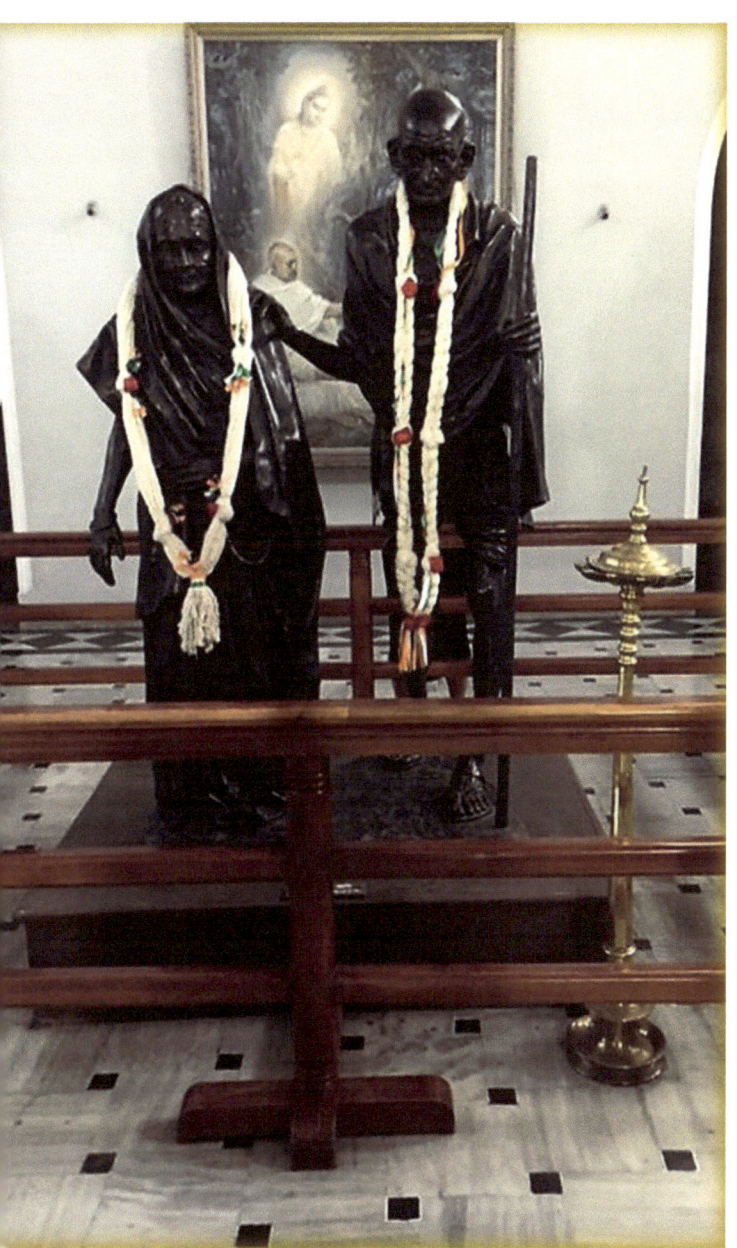

Mr. & Mrs. Gandhi, Aga Khan Palace | fig. 29

The Palace was constructed by Aga Khan III in 1892 and is considered a significant landmark in Indian history. The palace was an act of philanthropy by the Aga Khan to assist the poor dwelling in the neighboring areas of Pune, who were drastically hit by famine. Legend has it that the Aga Khan built the palace to provide employment to the famine-struck villagers of the surrounding region; the Aga Khan employed 1000 people, and the palace was constructed in five years' time.

The majestic Aga Khan Palace is one of the great marvels of India and became closely linked to the Indian Freedom Movement after it served as 'house-arrest incarceration' for Gandhi, his wife Kasturba, and his secretary Mahadev Desai - all were interned in the palace from August 1942 to May 1944, following the launch of Quit India Movement.

Kasturba and Mahadev Desai died during their period of palace captivity. Gandhi and Kasturba each have memorials located in the same complex, facing the Mula River.

In 1969, Aga Khan Palace was donated to the Indian people by Aga Khan IV as a mark of respect to Gandhi and his philosophy and today houses a prominent memorial to Gandhi. In 2003 Archaeological Survey of India declared Aga Khan Palace a monument of national importance. The Palace is maintained by Gandhi National Memorial Society

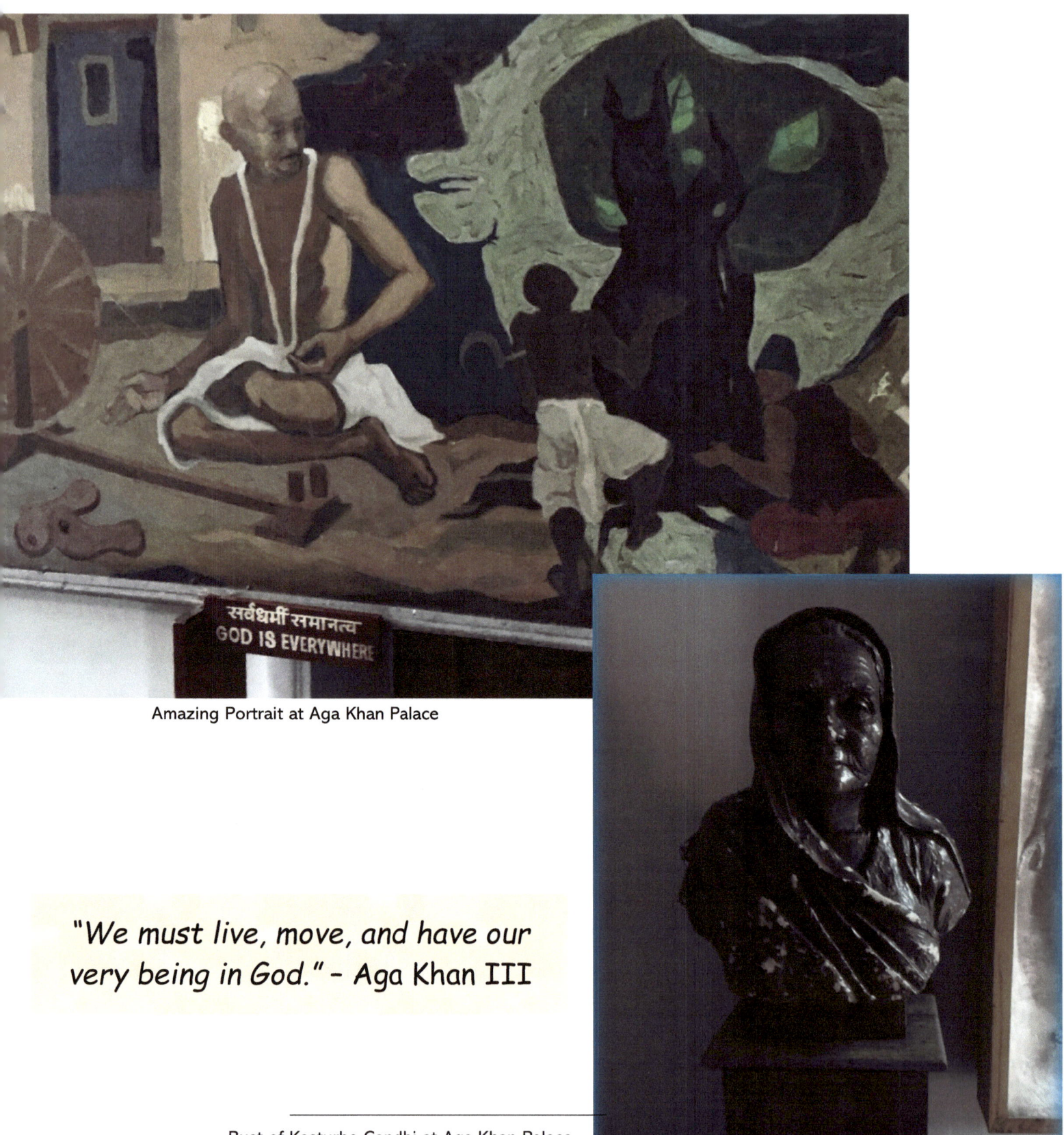

Amazing Portrait at Aga Khan Palace

"We must live, move, and have our very being in God." – Aga Khan III

Bust of Kasturba Gandhi at Aga Khan Palace

Return to Mumbai, Old Mumbai & MarketPlace/SHARE…

The Great Indian Sage Vivekananda greets all who enter Mumbai | Lynnea Bylund

Skilled artisan of MarketPlace/SHARE | fig. 30

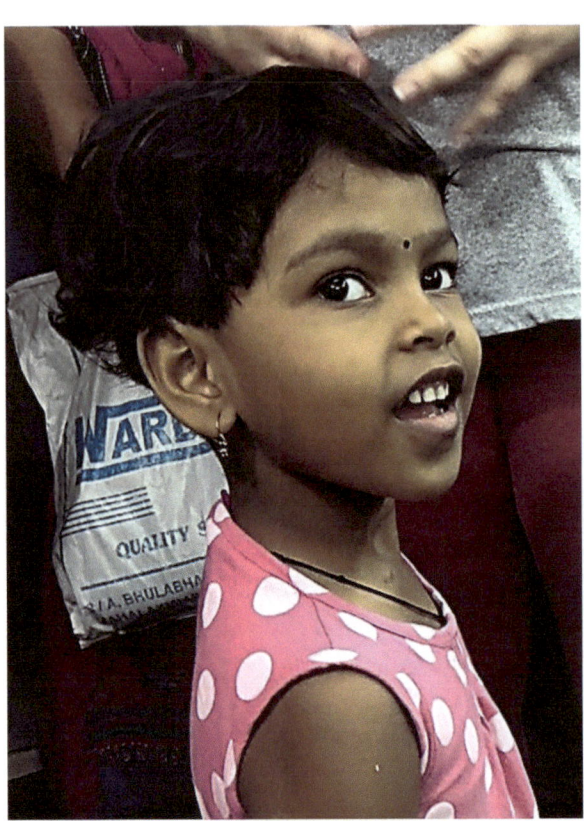
Happy outside MarketPlace/SHARE | fig. 31

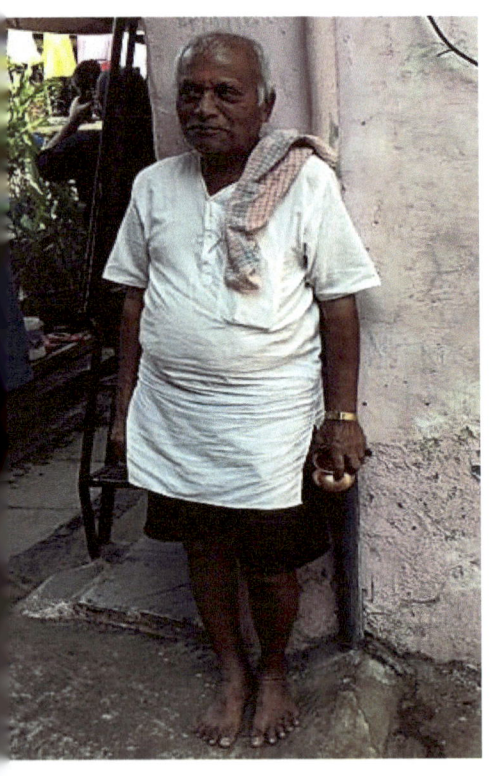
Vendor outside MarketPlace/SHARE | fig. 32

Devastating 2009 Monsoon, Mumbai | fig. 33

> *"You must not lose faith in humanity. Humanity is an ocean; if a few drops of the ocean are dirty, the ocean does not become dirty."* - Gandhi

MUMBAI – MARKETPLACE/SHARE

MarketPlace/SHARE (MPS} is an innovative fair trade and not-for-profit organization established by Pushpika Freitas in 1986, which combines the experience of running a business with a variety of support programs designed to effect real, meaningful, and lasting change in the lives of low-income women in India.

MPS grew out of a very small-scale venture organized in 1980 to help three low-income women in Mumbai, India. Today MPS (also known as 'Handwork of India') has grown to over 500 artisans who are organized into 14 independent co-operatives which produce high-quality women's apparel and home decor. The slums of Mumbai are full of women who need to support their families but face obstacles, including poor education, cultural barriers, and religious restrictions.

Empowered with independence and self-confidence, these women become agents of change; and they find the courage, with support of their cooperative members, to fight for what they believe.

During the 2009-2010 Legacy Tour of India, the delegation visited Handwork of India after a devastating monsoon ripped through their offices and the slum communities they serve. They lost all shortly before the big 2010 earthquake in Haiti.

Artisan fabric loom, MPS | fig. 34

> When the MarketPlace/Share community heard the news of Haiti, and how it devastated the people, they decided as a community that everything they made and sold for one month would be donated to Haiti earthquake relief, and despite their own struggles!

GANDHI & TRAIN TRAVEL

Gandhi exiting a train in 'Bombay' Mahatma receives a donation | Figs. 35 & 36

Gandhi 'traveled extensively throughout India, mostly on trains. The main purpose of such journeys, as he had said himself, was "to get a grasp of the life" in India. Gandhi authored a book, consisting of 6 essays, the first one titled "Third Class In Indian Railways." He talks about poverty in India, especially apparent when traveling on trains across India. Gandhi felt that government officials should be required to ride in third class.

Gandhi's final journey by train was on the 'Asthi Special, which took his remains for submersion in the rivers at Prayag near the confluence of the Ganges and Yamuna rivers at Allahabad and required five third class carriages.

Without a doubt, the ideal way to see India is not on a plane, but on the ground via the incredible Indian railway system. No visit to India is complete without experiencing the hustle and bustle of Indian train depots and a safe journey aboard an Indian express train with the tea peddler's welcome cry of "Chai, chai, garam chai" wafting down the aisle.

"I travel third class because there is no fourth class." -Gandhi

Salt worker in the 'Little Rann' Kutch-desert views us with caution | Mat Fuller

TRAVELING THROUGH KUTCH
by Kasturi Gandhi
(Gandhi Great-Great Granddaughter)

Kutch Village Life | figs. 37-39

Kutch (also spelled as 'Kachchh') is a district within the Gujarat state in western India with its capital at Bhuj, and it is the single largest district of India. As a traveler through Kutch, you'll find that it matches the common notion of rural India: Herds of camels, buffaloes and goats trudge the highway with turbaned bidi-puffing men; the air carries dust and the wooden clack-clack sound of handlooms at work; lines of fluttering indigo and madder-dyed fabric color the village courtyards; and women with heavily pierced ears and tattooed arms often sit embroidering at the doorsteps of their homes.

When I arrived in Kutch in 2016, I was immediately smitten by these scenes. I was there to document recycled plastic weaving, a project undertaken by the women of a village called Awadh Nagar. But working with them and staying back in the district for another year showed me the stories behind the rural imagery - stories of loss, courage and resilience.

It was in Kutch that I truly understood what my great-great grandfather 'Bapu' was referring to when he said, "The future of India lies in its villages." In Kutch I was able to see in practice a lot of Bapu's thoughts, which I had only read as excerpts or quotes before. Through this piece, I'd like to share with you my experiences with the Kutchi communities and their collaborators, and the lessons of ingenuity, courage, peace and non-violence they taught me throughout.

To give you some context, Kutch has a diverse ecosystem of grasslands, mangroves, and a large salt desert. Over centuries, owing to the natural resources abundantly available there, it has become the perfect home for artisan and rustic communities. It sits, however, on a sensitive geographical zone, and has suffered some of India's worst earthquakes.

On India's Republic (Constitution) Day in 2001, a 7.7 magnitude earthquake had its epicenter in Bhuj, the central town of Kutch, and left thousands dead in its wake. It also struck a violent blow to the homegrown cottage industries that had seen rapid rise in the villages.

Round Bhunga Homes, inside & out, the Kutch | fig. 34 & 35

Volunteers and field experts who arrived at the scene realized that a wholesome solution was needed once the immediate relief work was carried out. Some of them came together to create Kutch Nav specialized organizations

One of those specialized organizations was the Hunnarshala, a group of architecture and infrastructure specialists who possessed extensive knowledge and experience in post-earthquake community rehabilitation. They saw that the worst affected were structures with angles, basically all the square and rectangle buildings.

Traditionally in Kutch, however, homes were made with a circular base and shape. The Hunnarshala team saw this as the perfect opportunity to bring back the circular house or 'bhunga.' The bhungas would be built, it was decided, by the residents themselves. Hunnarshala created kits containing the building tools for 200 villages, which were to be shared within the community.

They also provided compressed-earth to the people to create the bhungas with. This way, the rehabilitation process became shared, eco-friendly, sustainable, and self-sufficient. Today, even though the tremors persist, the bhungas stand sturdily in the villages. I spent many afternoons interviewing, eating lunch and sipping chai in these bhungas, and can attest that they have a unique beauty and comfort.

Over the years Hunnarshala built its own home and headquarters near Bhuj, the central town of Kutch, from where they raised several infrastructural projects post-earthquake.

Exquisite leather craft of the Kutch | Fig. 36

During my time in the Kutch, I enjoyed the good fortune of having as friends volunteers from Hunnarshala, and each one was associated with an inspiring project.

One was working on a slum rehabilitation project - in which each home was designed and built along with the resident, typically a shop-vendor, auto rickshaw driver, or mason.

Unlike government-style village recuperation, these homes could be customized per the needs of the resident.

The basis of this was 'incrementality', whereby the resident could add features to their home at a later date whenever they had the means to. For example, they could opt for a ground floor, one bathroom and a fence, as per their power to spend at present, and could allow for future add-ons.

Another friend, who had worked on an architectural thesis about applying Gandhian principles to post-riot rehabilitation, was working with survivors of communal riots in a town in central India, to build homes for them in a new village where they felt safer. These homes, too, were built collaboratively, encouraging plenty of community spaces to increase human engagement - a necessary process in recovery.

"The future of India lies in its villages." – Gandhi

Deeper into the Kutch, and Hunnarshala …

Hunnarshala-trained artisan weaving a traditional 'charpai' (bed), Kutch | figs. 37 - 39

> *"The best way to find yourself is to lose yourself in the service of others."* – Gandhi

BHUJ, KUTCH -

HUNNARSHALA FOUNDATION

Hunnarshala Foundation was created after the devastating Kutch earthquake of 2001 to build sustainable homes for urban and rural populations. Since then it has been offering knowledge and skills for building designs, settlement planning, social housing, disaster reconstruction, wastewater treating systems and infrastructure development.

The Foundation offers a two-year course for school dropouts, teaching carpentry and masonry skills. They in turn work to convert urban slums into organized efficient townships. Hunnarshala's philosophy arose from projects that were successfully demonstrating that processes controlled and managed by the people themselves can work well. This concept of people managing the processes had already been demonstrated successfully in other sectors like crafts, savings & (micro) credits.

Hunnarshala building techniques, the Kutch | figs. 41-43

Hunnarshala-built home with open kitchen | fig. 40

Hunnarshala rebuilt this earthquake-damaged neighborhood | fig. 44

Happy new home owner & Hunnarshala builder crew | figs. 45 & 46

"To a true artist only the face is beautiful, quite apart from its exterior, and shines with the truth within the soul." – Gandhi

KUKMA, KUTCH –
KHAMIR RESOURCE CENTER

KHAMIR stands for Kutch Heritage, Art, Music, Information & Resources. KHAMIR also means 'intrinsic pride' in 'Kutchi,' the local language. KHAMIR works to strengthen and promote the rich artisanal traditions of the Kutch district. At present, villagers are quite prosperous and have notable presence. There is enough penetration of telephone, and all houses have electricity and water.

Started in 2005 with funding from the Nehru Foundation for Development, KHAMIR serves as a platform for the promotion of traditional handicrafts and allied cultural practices, the processes involved in their creation, and the preservation of culture, community and local environments.

Traditional arts & crafts of the Kutch | figs. 47-49

Dying the jeet prior to weaving | fig. 50

Ready for weaving | fig. 51

Clay water pot in jeet macramé | fig. 52

Wall mural of traditional attire Kutch wife | fig. 53

"Poverty is the worst form of violence." – Gandhi

SALT BEDS OF KUTCH

The salt beds of the Little Rann (little desert) of Kutch showcase the plight of the salt panning workers who are exploited by a cartel of salt traders and unprotected by an unsympathetic Gujarat-state government administration.

We see the harsh working conditions in the salt pans and witness the salt workers gathering salt through arduous hard labor.

From young childhood to old age, denizens of the Little Rann toil doggedly in the salt beds, "harvesting" salt by gathering and drying the endless supply of salty brine sludge that seeps up through the desert floor of what was once a sea; providing nearly three-quarters of India's demand.

Crystal plucked from dried salt marsh, Little Rann Kutch | fig. 54

Harsh beauty, sun setting over salt beds | fig. 55

Endless salt brings endless toil to the salt worker | Fig. 58

Father & son salt workers and their humble abode | figs. 56-57

The hard cracked ground of the summer Rann | fig. 60

Proud motorcycle owner enjoys a rare mobility in the Rann | fig. 59

Next stop - Gujarat Vidyapith in Ahmedabad, "The Gandhi University"…

Iconic entrance to Gujarat Vidyapith | Fig. 61

Arun mounts a science fair power-generator cycle | Fig. 62

India PM Nehru visits Gujarat Vidyapith, 1949 | Fig. 64

> "An education, which does not teach us to discriminate between good and bad, to assimilate the one and eschew the other, is a misnomer" – Gandhi

AHMEDABAD - GUJARAT VIDYAPITH

Classroom for mechanical cotton-spinning tech. | Fig. 66

Gujarat Vidyapith, the university founded by Gandhi in 1920, provides higher education with a blend of courses ranging from beginner horticulture to advanced doctorate programs.

The main objective is to develop future citizens of character, skill, culture, and dedication for the conduct of all movements connected with the regeneration of India in accordance with ideals taught and lived by Gandhi himself.

Gandhian guiding principles of Gujarat Vidyapith are:
- Adherence to truth and non-violence.
- Participation in 'productive dignity' of labor.
- Equality of all religions.
- Village dwellers given priority in all curricula.

The Gujarat Vidyapith education system includes regular participation in community work, social service, community prayer, simple and self-reliant living, study tours and field studies, hand spinning and training in craft work.

A chief focus of the Gujarat Vidyapith are experiments in various fields of education with a view to develop the application of Gandhian thought and practice in all aspects of education that involves the hand, the head and the heart.

Mural of Gandhi's signature 'charkha' (spinning wheel) | Fig. 65

Students mingle on campus | Fig. 67

Wall mural depicts equality of religions | Fig. 68

Students attend a Q&A with Legacy Tour delegates | Fig. 69

"I need no inspiration other than from Nature." - Gandhi

AHMEDABAD – SABARMATI ASHRAM

We see that wherever Gandhi spent his time, it has become a place of pilgrimage; and wherever he roamed has become a sanctified location. The Sabarmati Ashram is located in the Sabarmati suburb of Ahmedabad, so named after the holy river Sabarmati on whose banks it sits, is such an example. This site no longer functions as a working ashram but as a museum and an institution whose aim is to preserve and propagate the legacy of 'Mahatma.'

Gandhi lived at the Sabarmati Ashram with his wife Kasturba for over 12 years, from 1917 to 1930. Gandhi led the famous Satyagraha Salt March to Dandi from this base; and he established the Gujarat University while living at Sabarmati. The spinning wheel used by Gandhi himself and the writing table remains in his room at the ashram.

Visitors from around the world arrive daily with curiosity and feelings of devotion and feel inspired and enlivened. More than half a million visit Sabarmati Ashram every year. The Ashram is a source of inspiration for the present generation and will serve as such for generations to come. Indeed, Gandhi's ideals serve as a beacon for all.

Sabarmati entry plaque | Fig. 70

Gandhi's private quarters at Sabarmati | Fig.71

"Sabarmati is right for a search for truth and fearlessness; on the one side are the iron bolts of the British foreigners' jail, and on the other side the thunderbolts of unrelenting nature."

Sabarmati, flanked between a Jail and a crematory, Gandhi was known to say this.

Captured at Sabarmati Ashram | Figs. 73-76

Radiant Happiness!

The Ashram where Gandhi lived 1917-30 | Fig. 72

Gandhi greets all who enter | Fig. 80

Arun gives Grandfather's 'charkha' a spin | Fig. 78

Ashram Museum entrance sign | Fig. 79

Equality of Faiths, Tushar Gandhi art hangs at the Ashram | Fig. 77

"Satyagraha has been designed as an effective substitute for violence."
- Gandhi -

Mural in the Ashram visitor center depicting Gandhi leading the Dandi Salt March | Fig. 82

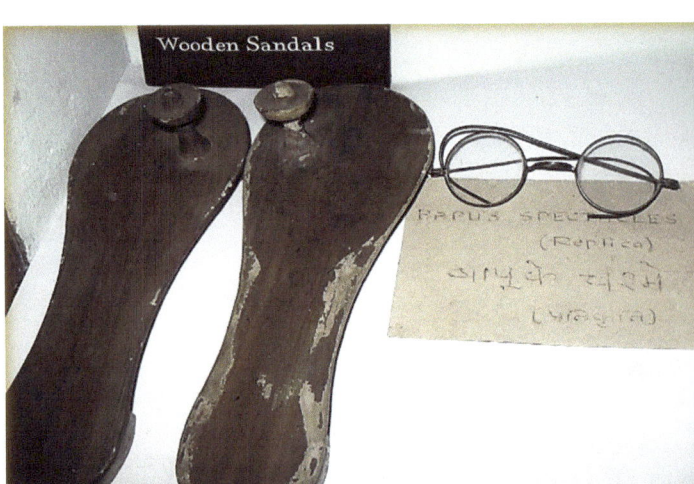

Sandals and glasses of the Mahatma | Fig. 83

Three weary travelers, Tushar Gandhi w/ Lynnea & Arun | Fig. 81

- March 12, 1930 -
Independence protesters begin marching 240 miles, from Ahmedabad to Dandi, intending to defy British law and produce their own salt from the seawater. This was Gandhi's Salt March, a peaceful salvo in the fight for India independence.

Gandhi initially moved to the Sabarmati to practice organic food growing strategies; it stood between a jail and crematory. The Ashram has stood witness to many important events that were instrumental in shaping the Mahatma and 'Bapu' of a nation.

Gandhi's Prayer memorialized at Sabarmati | Fig. 84

[47]

On to Ganeshpura, Ahmedabad and S.E.W.A. ...

Oxen in India are a scared symbol of health and abundance. Revered as a consecrated animal, they often roam undisturbed.

Magnificent 'Holy Ox' greets our arrival to Ganeshpura | Fig. 85

"In a gentle way you can shake the world." -Gandhi

AHMEDABAD – S.E.W.A.

SEWA (Self Employed Women's Association) originated in 1972 as the women's wing of Textile Labour Association (TLA, established by Gandhi in 1918. It is an organization of poor, self-employed women who earn a living through their own labor and small businesses. They do not obtain regular salaried employment with welfare benefits like workers in the organized sector. They fall within the unprotected labor forces of India. Constituting 93% of the labor force, yet their work is not counted and hence remains unavailable to worker benefits, hence the miraculous SEWA union.

Gandhi Legacy India Tour has been visiting SEWA in Ahmedabad for over a decade. Over the years we've had the pleasure of meeting with several women empowered in SEWA leadership.

SEWA ladies of Ganeshpura great us with lunch | Figs. 86 & 87

We're always greeted at SEWA with love and blessings, and then given a passionate presentation of various projects they've initiated, a tour of SEWA H.Q., and a visit to the local community SEWA Bank.

> SEWA gave our Gandhi group a broad overview of their history and honorable accomplishments, along with field tours, in order that we might be best able to share first hand experiences of the solutions they've implemented and to address the panoply of community needs.

S.E.W.A.'s Ela Bhatt inspects a day's output | Fig. 88

Skilled S.E.W.A. artisans work a design | Fig. 89

THE S.E.W.A. SUCCESS
by Dr. Margaret McLaren
Dept. of Philosophy | Rollins College

SEWA founder Ela Bhatt | Fig. 91

The SEWA success story began with a struggle around economic issues but has grown to address many other challenges. The Self-Employed Women's Association was founded in 1972 by Gandhian-activist and civil-rights leader Ela Bhatt of Ahmedabad. The organization is influenced by the ideas and philosophy of Gandhi; especially on the subjects of dignity of labor, importance of human values, and non-violence. Since its modest beginning in '72, SEWA's membership is now a million strong and growing.

SEWA's primary focus is to organize women workers in the informal sector, including capacity building, leadership training, organizing against police harassment and for fair wages, and access to sustainable income. From these economic challenges SEWA's work now encompasses a range of issues and projects, including cooperatives for: dairy, midwives, vendors, textile, block printing, and artisans.

Cheering the Ratification of S.E.W.A. 1972 | Fig. 90

> "Catching up to western economic models will turn us into incompetent followers. But if we address the realities of our own country, we will create change that makes us leaders of our own unique destiny."
> – Ela Bhatt

SEWA Cooperative Bank & H.Q. | Fig. 92

SEWA also provides a variety of projects and services for members, including a research center, a video project that trains the women to produce films to tell their own stories, an insurance office, a childcare center, and a publications office. SEWA helps poor, workingwomen to organize into cooperatives and unions to utilize their collective power.

Throughout all of its work SEWA employs a partnership model with poor women, responding to their needs and developing leadership from within the community. I learned about SEWA firsthand when I visited the SEWA office in Ahmedabad, Gujarat in January 2006 as part of a Gandhi Legacy Tour focusing on social justice.

Our group, led by Dr. Arun Gandhi, the fifth grandson of Mohandas K. (Mahatma) Gandhi, spent the day at the SEWA offices. We learned about the history and the mission of the organization, met many SEWA members, toured the office, sat in on a meeting, and heard a talk by SEWA's founder, Ela Bhatt. The next day our group had a free day, most went to a famous textile museum. I was so impressed with SEWA I asked if I could return.

I did return, and spent another day learning about various SEWA programs, visiting the Video SEWA unit, learning about an experiential immersion program where policy-makers, both foreign and domestic, live with a rural family to learn about the SEWA's projects and their impact on SEWA members.

I spent time with SEWA's researchers who work closely with members and help to influence national and international policy with their studies of SEWA's work. I met more SEWA members, who seemed to come in to the SEWA offices, bank, and project units in an ever-flowing stream. Women laughed, talked, joked, worked, and drank tea. It was clear that everyone felt comfortable, and that the relationships among them were easy and mutual. One indication of this is that regardless of role, rank, or caste SEWA members call each other "sister"; and while this is a respectful form of referring to someone in Gujarati, it is not typically done across divisions of caste and social hierarchies. The energy, excitement, and commitment to shared projects and goals were palpable. The women I have met through SEWA are truly inspirational; they embody the 'Gandhian change' that the world needs.

"Everything in India attracts me. It has everything that a human being with the highest possible aspirations can want." - Gandhi

OLD AHMEDABAD
- THE HERITAGE WALK

The historic walled city of Old Ahmedabad features some of the finest Indian-Islamic monuments and exquisite Hindu, Jain and Muslim temples. Its carved wooden houses are another unique architectural traditions. The full experience of Old Ahmedabad requires a guided walk through the 'Walled City' to truly observe its rich varied design, its art, religious places, its culture and traditions.

Friendly inquisitive young people, Old Ahmedabad | Fig. 93

The 'Old City' is uniquely comprised of hundreds of 'pols', enclaves of neighborhoods, and the pols are traversed by narrow lanes, typically terminating at a 'chowk' (marketplace) and a 'chabutro' (for nesting and feeding pigeons). Pols are protected by gates, cul-de-sacs and hidden passages, as discovered throughout our walk.

Elephant carries a hopeful vendor and his wares | Fig. 94

Old Ahmedabad provided us with a morning 'Heritage Walk' tour through numerous social, spiritual & historical areas of the 'Walled City.'

The Walled City, with 12 gates and numerous mosques, temples and towers, was founded in 1411. Its aged condition, the Indian Islamic design and the houses adorned with intricate wood carvings attest to a prior affluence.

Old Ahmedabad Heritage Walk | Figs. 95-97

Traditional chabutro for birds | Fig. 98

Historic temple sites abound | Figs. 99 & 100

On to meet the 'Solar Mamas' of Barefoot College in Tilonia, Ajmer…

Solar tech students learning to electrify their village | Fig. 102

Campus sign circa 1980 | Fig. 101

> *"Non-violence cannot be built on a factory civilization, but it can be built on self-contained villages."* – Gandhi

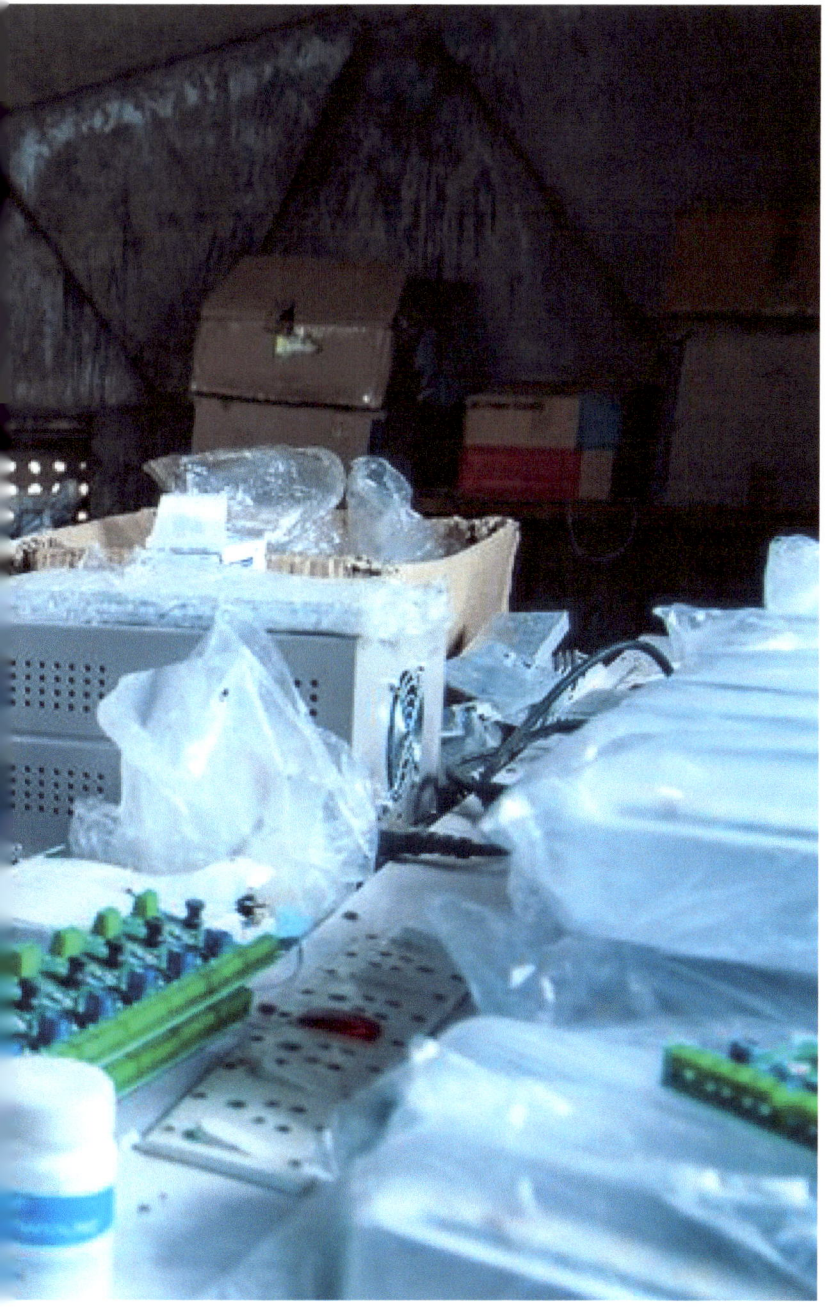

TILONIA, AJMER –
BAREFOOT COLLEGE

Established in 1972 by Bunker Roy in Tilonia, a small village in Rajasthan's Ajmer district, Barefoot College India is a women-centered organization that provides basic services and solutions to rural communities, with the objective of making them self-sufficient and sustainable. These 'Barefoot College solutions' can be broadly categorized into fields of education, skill development, health, drinking water, women empowerment, and electrification through solar.

Barefoot College believes that for any rural development activity to be successful and sustainable, it must be based in the villages, as well as managed and owned by those it serves.

All Barefoot initiatives whether social, political or economic, are planned and implemented by a network of rural men and women who are known as 'Barefoot Professionals'. Rural men and women irrespective of age, who are barely literate or even not at all, and without hope of getting even the lowest jobs, are becoming teachers, health workers, solar engineers, computer trainers, accountants, and more.

Barefoot 'Solar Mamas' display their wares | Figs. 103-105

The story of …
SANJIT 'BUNKER' ROY -&-
HIS BAREFOOT COLLEGE

Bunker Roy giving his Ted Talk

"With his abiding compassion for the rural poor in his native India, Bunker Roy has nurtured a grass-roots social entrepreneurship that is redefining the way the world thinks about fighting poverty," wrote Time Magazine in 2010 when Roy was included in its '100 Most Influential People of the World.'

As a college student from a privileged city background, Roy volunteered to spend his summer vacation working with famine victims in one of India's poorest states.

This early service involvement transformed Roy, and he committed himself to fight poverty and inequality. In 1972 he founded the Social Work and Research Centre (now known as Barefoot College) to demystify technology and put it to good use in the hands of poor communities. This radically simple approach to ending poverty, by tapping the wisdom, skills and resourcefulness of the poor themselves, is less expensive and more successful than approaches that rely on conventional external experts.

According to Roy, the formal system of education demeans and devalues proven traditional knowledge and practical wisdom that the poor value. Roy says his real education started in Tilonia, in the Ajmer district, when he worked as an unskilled laborer — blasting wells for water. "I lived with very poor and ordinary people under the stars and heard the stories they had to tell of their skills, knowledge, and wisdom that books and colleges cannot teach."

> "My real education began when I saw amazing rural villagers, water diviners, healers and midwives, at work - that marked the true beginning of the Barefoot College."

Roy started with a list of least-developed countries at the UN and launched "Solar Mamas," a 6-month program training rural women to become community solar-electrification engineers. The Barefoot solar training program brings uneducated middle-aged women together from around the world to become solar engineers and self-sufficient professionals. After a 6-month training program, these women return to their communities and "solar electrify" their villages as Roy calls it; a decentralized electrification solution for village households.

Arun & Bunker share a momentary respite | Fig. 106

The College follows the applied philosophies of M.K. Gandhi: Students eat, sleep, and work on the floor. They can stay for 20 years, or they can go home tomorrow. As of 2018, Barefoot College had trained over 1500 solar electrification engineers from nearly 2000 villages in over 60 countries; and Barefoot's 'Solar Mamas' have electrified more than 120,000 homes.

Electrical circuitry 101, Barefoot style | Fig.107

Bunker Roy challenged the system, putting localized Gandhian theory into practice before a global stage; and he reminded the world that Mahatma Gandhi is more relevant today than ever.

"Strengthen the rural areas and fewer people will migrate to the squalid urban centers. Give villagers the respect, opportunity, and self-confidence they need and they'll never move to urban slums."
— Bunker Roy

Determined vendor selling produce in Old Ahmedabad | Mat Fuller

Meet the Waterman of Rajasthan, the "Gandhi of Water" …

"Water, air, the land and the earth itself are not an birth right from our forefathers but on loan from our children."
– Gandhi

Tushar Gandhi, with Arun and the Waterman join villagers to view a newly dug 'johad' | Fig. 108

"Love is the subtlest force in the world." – Gandhi

As Waterman Singh explains...
"Water collects behind the crescent shaped johad-dams and nature takes over. The stored water slowly seeps into the soil, replenishing the groundwater beneath. The waters, then stored within the johads, are slowly percolated into fields in order to grow crops."

RAJASTHAN –

WATERMAN OF INDIA

Rajendra Singh is a man on a mission – to stop a 'third world war' from breaking over water shortages. Singh, known as the "Waterman of India," is a celebrated 'water reclamationist' from the Alwar district of Rajasthan India. In 2015 Singh won the Stockholm Water Prize, an award known as the "Nobel Prize for Water." The prize honors individuals, organizations and institutions whose work contributes to the conservation and protection of water resources, and to the well-being of the planet and its inhabitants.

Singh confesses that the foundation of his work is based on love, and not on formal environmental water education. He shares from the heart, "Love comes with the real action of nature. Love opens our hearts, so nothing is hidden. I do not know water engineering, water science, or water chemistry. I'm not an expert of water science, but love teaches all aspects of water in a simple way."

"I did not read the books on water science or water physics, never did I read a book on that matter as I began this work. By simply doing and seeing based in love we learned and now we as a community understand the water."

WATERMAN SAYS
"When many johads are built in a single area, they have a cumulative effect, resulting in the replenishment of entire aquifers."

Traditional crescent-shaped johads | Figs. 109 - 112

Waterman's NGO...

TARUN BHARAT SANGH

Waterman of India | Fig. 113

Waterman's organization in Rajasthan, Tarun Bharat Sangh (TBS), does ecological research and land development to provide clean fresh water to people. The organization was founded in 1975 by students and professors from University of Rajasthan.

In 1985 the direction of the organization changed when four young members of the organization went to live in the rural area of Alwar to teach rural children and do rural development. Of those four, only Rajendra Singh stayed on. Singh asked the local people what they needed most, and their answer - greater access to clean water.

Singh organized the building of a traditional rainwater collection and storage dam known as a 'johad, and with this first community johad, Singh changed the path of TBS towards development and never looked back.

Today, TBS is a champion in the sphere of "rain-water harvesting" and water reclamation, having constructed over 12,000 johads and related rainwater harvesting infrastructure with help from affected villagers and gracious donors.

This exemplifies "rain-water harvesting." Community members are accomplishing this on their own with hard work under the leadership of Singh, and without government support. Increasingly village communities now actively practice water harvesting and self-sufficiency.

A popular Tarun Bharat Sangh story - Singh once dissuaded a local band of thieves from stealing water, reforming and inspiring the bandits; and they subsequently traded their guns for shovels to dig new johads. The bandits were once wanted by the police but are now warmly invited into their homes and respected for the new water that they helped to provide.

TARUN BHARAT SANGH

Vandana Shiva and the Navdanya Farm-Institute, Dehradun …

Magnificent Oxen plow the fields of Navdanya
as foraging Egrets keep pace | Fig. 114

"The earth provides enough to satisfy every man's need, but never enough for every man's greed." -Gandhi

DEHRADUN – NAVDANYA and DR. VANDANA SHIVA

One of the more intriguing, but infrequent stops on our Gandhian mission (it is not included in the most current itinerary) is the Navdanya Institute in Dehradun, founded and led by Dr. Vandana Shiva. In 1982, she established the Research Foundation for Science, Technology and Ecology which in 1991 became Navdanya, "a national movement to protect the diversity and integrity of living resources, especially native seed, the promotion of organic farming and fair trade."

Vandana Shiva is a world-renowned and thought-provoking Gandhian advocate in many regards: She is a scientist and philosopher, with degrees in Philosophy of Science and Physics. She is also an environmental warrior-activist, fighting to preserve biodiversity, particularly crop biodiversity, and an adherent of 'eco-feminism' - which connects the exploitation and domination of women with the unrestrained exploitation of the environment.

The mission of Vandana Shiva's Navdanya is to promote peace and harmony, justice and sustainability. Navdanya strives to achieve these goals through the conservation, renewal and rejuvenation of the gifts of biodiversity we have received from nature and our ancestors, and to defend these gifts as "commons." The setting up of community seed banks is central to Navdanya's mission of regenerating nature's (and people's) wealth. Keeping seeds, biodiversity and traditional knowledge in people's hands to generate livelihoods and provide basic needs is Navdanya's core program for the elimination of poverty.

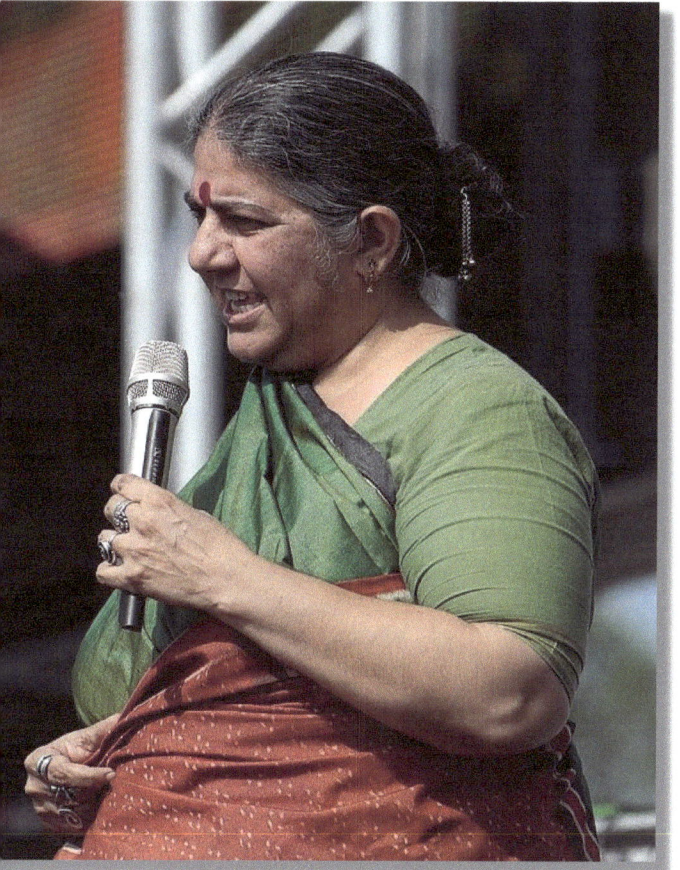

Vandana Shiva | Figs. 115 & 116

"Bright sun, good company, and we are always happy when Arun brings his Gandhi Legacy group to visit!"
- Dr. Shiva

Shiva's commitment and strong positions, developed over the past 40 years, have led her to become one of the major figures of environmental activism in the developing world. The expression "tree hugger", which refers to environmentalists, was coined after Shiva and other activists hugged trees to oppose commercial logging in Uttarakhand India in the 1970s. Her methods may have changed since, but the strength of her commitment remains intact.

Vandana Shiva shared with our group what wakes her up in the morning, keeps her going and takes her to bed at night ...

> "We combine deep engagement and best giving with detachment. We do not know where things may go - a Monsanto bribe can interfere in the middle of it all - or something else can happen and we know that the world is too complex to be influenced by our little intervention, no matter how big of a heart we come from. We must always combine our passion with detachment."

Dr. Shiva receives a gift of 'Not Two Is Peace' | Fig. 117

Shiva w/samplings of Navdanya's Seedbank Storage | Fig. 118

- SHIVA'S 'SEED SATYAGRAHA' -
"The seed bank at Navdanya conserves and cultivates thousands of crop varieties. Navdanya has saved 4,000 rice species, 2,200 varieties of oilseeds, cereals, pulses, vegetables, millets, 200 varieties of wheat and 150 species of fruit."

Sadly, Bapu appears to have predicted his own death by assassin's bullet just 48 hours prior.

"If I am to die by the bullet of a madman, I just do so smiling. There must be no anger within me. God must be in my heart and on my lips."
— Gandhi (1/28/1948)

"The law of sacrifice is uniform throughout the world, and it demands the sacrifice of the bravest and the most spotless."
— Gandhi

The Birla House in New Delhi,
where Gandhi's life-journey ended ...

Birla House Prayer Grounds, one of 11 installations worldwide of the World Peace Gong, displaying all nations' flags Fig. 120

Old Birla House & Gandhi Smirti | Fig. 121

Birla Red Urn at the Eternal Gandhi Multimedia Exhibit, Birla House | Fig. 126

"Live as if you were to die tomorrow. Learn as if you were to live forever." – Gandhi

NEW DEHLI - BIRLA HOUSE

The Gandhi Smriti 'Remembrance' at the Old Birla House is the now-consecrated place where Mahatma Gandhi's epic life ended on January 30, 1948, in New Delhi. The final words from Gandhi's lips were Ram, Ram, Ram (a Hindu name for God).

Gandhi lived in the Birla House from early September 1947 to late January 1948; thus, the hallowed house captured many memories of the last 144 days of Gandhi's life. On January 12, 1948, Gandhi undertook a five-day fast to end Hindu and Muslim violence. Ten days previous to his death, on January 20, 1948, a previous failed assassination attempt occurred on the grounds.

Old Birla House was acquired by the India's national government in 1971 and was converted to a National Memorial (Smriti) of the Father of the Nation. It was opened to the public on August 15, 1973.

Preserved at Gandhi Smriti are the rooms where Gandhi lived and worked through his final day and the prayer grounds where he held a mass congregation each evening. It was on the prayer grounds where an assassin's bullets felled Gandhiji. The building and grounds have been preserved as they were in those days.

Memoriam Einstein Prayer Garden Rock | Fig. 122

जीवनके अंतिम दिन प्रार्थनास्थल की ओर
गांधीजीने इस पथ पर संचार किया

THE PATH ALONG WHICH GANDHI WALKED
TO THE PRAYER GROUND ON THE LAST DAY

Gandhi Smriti &
Prayer Grounds
Figs. 123–125

"Birth and death are not two different states, they are different aspects of the same state." -Gandhi

Cremation Memorial grounds | Fig. 127

NEW DEHLI –

RAJ GHAT MEMORIAL

The Raj Ghat memorial is a black marble platform that marks the spot of Mahatma Gandhi's cremation on 31 January 1948, one day after his assassination. It is left open to the sky while an eternal flame burns perpetually at its head. It is located on the banks of the river Yamuna in Delhi.

A stone footpath flanked by lawns leads to the walled enclosure encompassing the memorial. All guests must remove their footwear before entering the Raj Ghat walls. Raj Ghat loosely translates to King's Bank (where King alludes to the importance of the place and Bank as in the shore of the Yamuna River). Raj Ghat also provides memorials to final samadhi and/or cremation spots of twelve other Indian leaders including Jawaharlal Nehru and Indira Gandhi.

Cremation Memorial components | Figs. 128-130

The Raj Ghat Memorial | Fig. 131

THREE FINAL & OPTIONAL HISTORIC STOPS…

Qutub Minar, the world's tallest brick and mortar structure – built 8 centuries ago it still stands strong.

Taj Mahal, an architectural conceptualization of both life on earth and in the heavens.

Red Fort of Agra, built at the peak of Mughal rule and combining Persian design with Indian tradition.

Historic final stops | Figs. 132-134

The world's tallest brick and mortar structure | Figs. 135-137

"The eyes do not see what the mind does not want." - Indian Proverb

DEHLI – THE QUTUB MINAR

The Qutub Minar is the tallest brick and mortar structure in the world. Incredibly, and despite having suffered a great many ravages of nature, the nearly 73 meter (238ft.) tower continues to stand erect after 8 centuries! The Minar was commissioned in 1199 by Qutubuddin Aibak ('Qutub'), an actual high-ranking 'Mamluk' (slave-warrior) and general of the Sultan Mohammed Ghauri. Ghauri successfully conquered northern India in 1192, and soon after returned to Ghur (now part of Afghanistan), appointing his trusted general/slave, Qutub, as governor of Delhi and de facto ruler of the Northern parts of India. After the untimely death of Ghauri, Qutub declared himself ruler and founded a new Mamluk dynasty.

Sunset through an Islamic arch | Fig. 138

Prior to the Minar, in 1192 Qutub commissioned the mosque 'Quwwat-ul-Islam' (Might of Islam), one of the oldest mosques in the north of India, and its construction utilized the dismantling and reassembling of 27 existing Hindu and Jain temples, which were richly decorated with statues of gods, goddesses, dancers, mythical figures and animals. Many or most of the re-cycled statues were defaced prior to being utilized for the new mosque, as Islam prohibits worshiping idolatrous figures.

Tombs at Qutub Minar | Figs. 140 & 141

Hindu deity, face intact | Fig 139

"The world believes it was built by love, but reading Shah Jahan's own words on the Taj Mahal, one could say it was grief that built it."
- Aysha Taryam

Taj Mahal on a glorious cloudless day | Fig. 142

"The Taj Mahal rises above the banks of the river like a solitary tear suspended on the cheek of time." – Rabindranath Tagore

AGRA - TAJ MAHAL

The Taj Mahal has been called, "a symbol for the whole nation" – it gives the Indian people their identity. The Taj Mahal is an architectural conceptualization of both life on earth and in the heavens, according to Islamic belief. Thus, an equal allowance of space was allocated to bazaars and sarais (courtyard-styled inns) facing the great gate, which was the representation of life on the earth.

The color scheme of the Taj Mahal is deeply symbolic. The worldly elements and other buildings are all clad in red sandstone while the mausoleum is in pristine white, representing purity.

Commissioned in 1632 by the Mughal emperor Shah Jahan as a shrine and tomb for his greatest love and deceased wife, Mumtaz Mahal, the Taj Mahal also houses the tomb of Shah Jahan himself. The main entrance arch frames the monument in such a way that it creates an optical illusion that as an observer moves closer, the Taj Mahal seems to grow smaller; and it seems to grow bigger as you walk backwards! An optical illusion was created into the building of the minarets as well – they were leaned slightly outwards so they would look perfectly vertical and would not seem to be converging at the top.

In 1643, when the Taj Mahal was finished – it had taken nearly 12 years for the more than 20,000 artisans to fulfill the vision of the Shah in stone.

"Taj Mahal is pinkish in the morning, milky white in the evening and golden when the moon shines; and on a sunny mid-day the Taj appears as a perfect pearl within an azure milieu - the effect is such as never experienced from any other work of art."
- UNKNOWN

The gateway entrance is located to the eastern side of Taj Mahal. It is a red sandstone structure inlaid with white marble and elaborate intricate carvings.

Three views of the Taj and its 'gateway' entrance | Figs. 143-145

The tombs of Shah Jahan and his beloved Mumtaz Mahal | Fig. 146

The 5th Sultan Mughal of India, Shah Jahan, built the Taj Mahal as a monument and tomb to his beloved wife Mumtaz Mahal, and he would also come to be entombed there.

Ganesha of marble & jewels | Fig. 147

View with minaret | Fig. 148

Portrait of a young Jahan, artist unknown | Fig. 149

Striking view of Agra Fort | Fig. 150

Planned by a Muslim king and built by Hindu masons, the imposing Agra Fort is the most visible testimony of Akbar the Great's rule.

> "You can chain me, torture me, you can even destroy this body, but you will never imprison my mind." – Gandhi

RED FORT OF AGRA

Agra Fort, standing two miles from the Taj Mahal, is a historical fort in the city of Agra, built in 1565. It was the main residence of the emperors of the Mughal Dynasty until 1638 when the Mughal capital was shifted from Agra to Delhi. Largely overshadowed by the nearby Taj Mahal, Agra Fort is one of the finest of all Mughal forts of India.

The Fort was built primarily as a military structure by Akbar the Great and was later transformed into a palace by his grandson, Shah Jahan, and it later became Jahan's gilded prison for eight years after Jahan's son, Shah Aurangzeb, seized power in 1658. Jahan was restricted to his personal 'Shah Burj' compound and was closely watched and was never again permitted to communicate with the outside world.

It is said that during his final years of imprisonment, Shah Jahan would either read the Quran or gaze at his beloved wife's memorial from the Shah Burj veranda; and this little corner was the only solace of his last days.

View from Shah Burj veranda | Fig. 151

During his final years, imprisoned within the Fort, Shah Jahan found continual solace in this view.

> From mighty fort of the Mughal dynasty to Northern India's most luxurious palace, and ultimately a gilded prison compound for the Shah Jahan

Morning up-close view of Fort | Fig. 152

Panorama of Agra Fort | Fig. 153

Farewell to India for now ...

Smiling Hindu Goddess bids us farewell at Delhi Airport | Fig. 154

The metallic art displays of Indira Gandhi International are imposing & astonishing

Elephants sculpture at Delhi Airport | Fig. 144

"I have watched the cultures of all lands blow around my house and other winds have blown the seeds of peace, for travel is the language of peace." -Gandhi

DEPARTING

INDIRA GANDHI INT'L

AKA 'Delhi Airport' is India's busiest air travel hub. And like the Mumbai airport, it's also a modern marvel – the first airport in the world to be registered under Clean Development Mechanism of United Nations Framework Convention on Climate Change – this international air hub has a solar plant within its landing fields.

Our final departing memories are of the display-art opulence the caliber of which is not often found at other International hubs

Artistic display of Namaskara
Sun Salute Yoga | Fig. 156

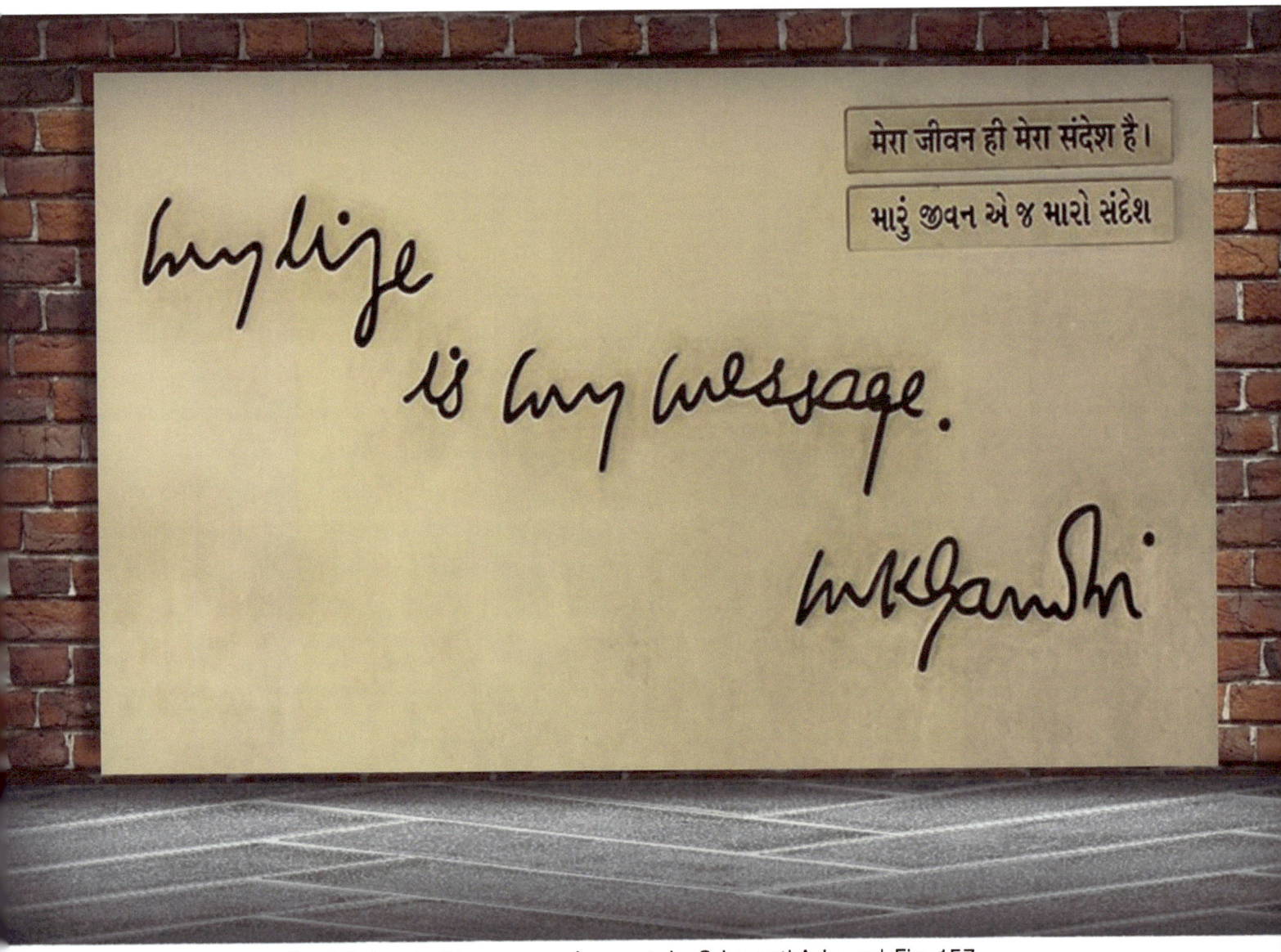

Gandhi's handwritten message hangs at the Sabarmati Ashram | Fig. 157

EPILOGUE – GANDHI'S 'TALISMAN OF RECALL'

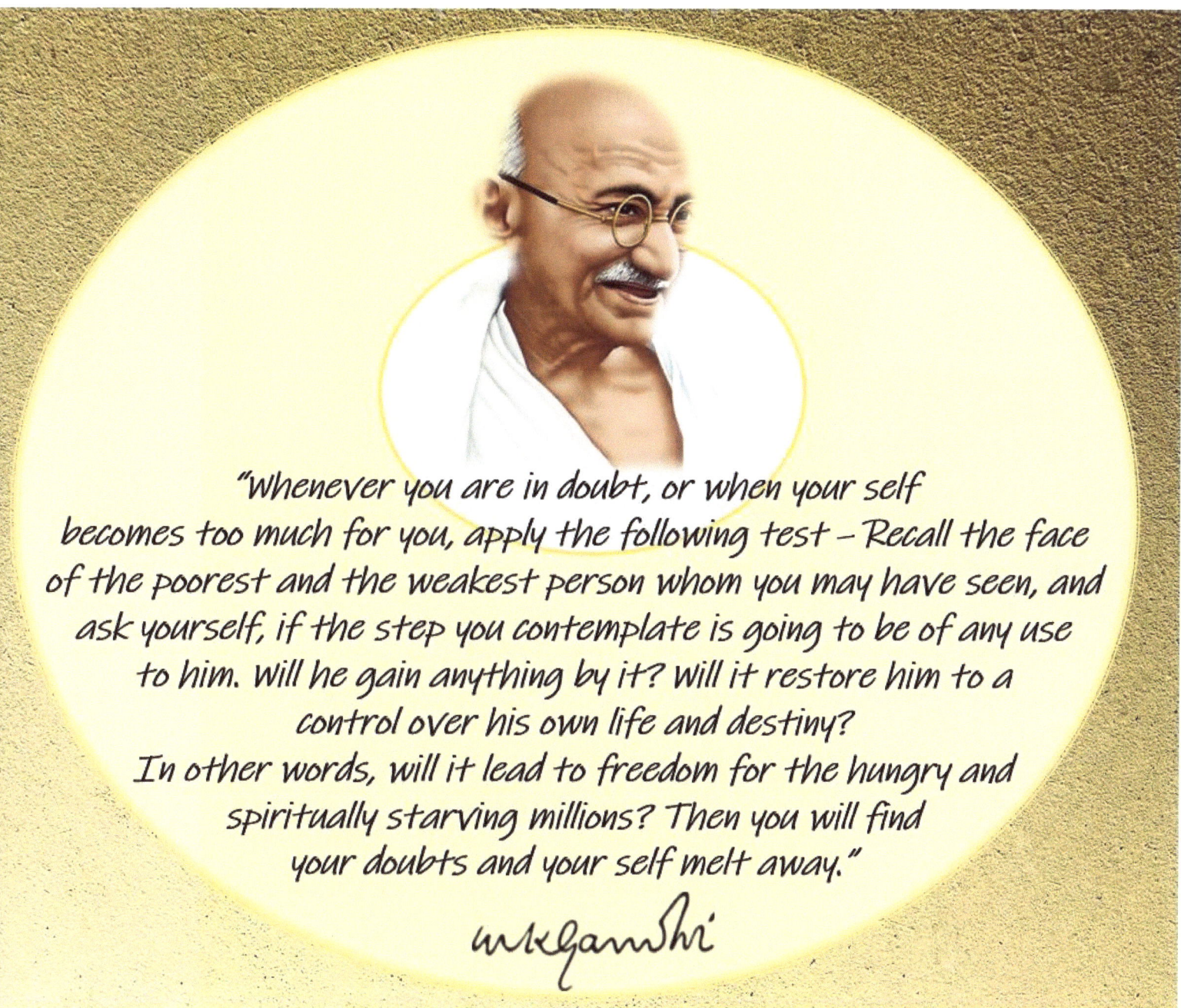

"Whenever you are in doubt, or when your self becomes too much for you, apply the following test – Recall the face of the poorest and the weakest person whom you may have seen, and ask yourself, if the step you contemplate is going to be of any use to him. Will he gain anything by it? Will it restore him to a control over his own life and destiny? In other words, will it lead to freedom for the hungry and spiritually starving millions? Then you will find your doubts and your self melt away."

— M K Gandhi

Legacy traveler assisting in Old Ahmedabad | Fig. 160

AVANI School class sand art | Fig. 159

AVANI School Eco Dome | Fig. 158

Peacock in the countryside of Delhi | Lynnea Bylund

The magnificent peacock is a common sight in India, where they are protected as the official national bird. Known as 'mayura' in Sanskrit, the peacock enjoys a fabled place in India and is oft depicted in temple art and mythology. In Indian Hindu and Buddhist traditions, peacocks also represent inspirational wisdom.

IMAGE CREDITS

PAGE	DESCRIPTION & SOURCE
vii	'Not-Two Is Peace', Adi Da Samraj	visit www.Da-Peace.com
viii-ix	Endless toil at the Kolhapur Brickyards	by Scott Kafora (own work)
xii	Smiling woman vendor in Old Ahmedabad	by Mat Fuller (own work)
1	AVANI student, Kolhapur	by Mat Fuller (own work)
2	Wise woman on the streets of Old Mumbai	by Mat Fuller (own work)
	Teenagers in Ahmedabad	by Mat Fuller (own work)
	Blessed by a child in Kolhapur	by Scott Kafora (own work)
	Spiritual renunciates in Old Mumbai	by Mat Fuller (own work)
3	Arun Gandhi takes an airborne respite	by Scott Kafora (own work)
5	Fig, 2 – AVANI student gesturing 'namaste', Kolhapur	by Scott Kafora (own work)
8-9	Fig. 3 – Indian art adorns Chhatrapati Shivaji corridor, Mumbai	by Trinidade, Wikimedia Commons
10	Fig. 4 – Mani Bhavan, Mumbai	by Lynnea Bylund (derivative of Jorge Láscar, Wikimedia Commons)
10-11	Fig. 5 – MLK Jr. in his office with Gandhi portrait	Bob Fitch Photography Archive, Stanford Library
11	Fig. 6 – Mani Bhavan, Hall of History	By Nicholas, Wikimedia Commons
12	Fig. 7 – Mani Bhavan, Gandhi's Private Quarters	by Dennis Jarvis, Wikimedia Commons
	Fig. 8 – Mani Bhavan entrance	by Dennis Jarvis, Wikimedia Commons
	Fig. 9 – Mani Bhavan entrance plaque	by Lynnea Bylund (own work)
13	Fig. 10 – Kumkum adorned Indian woman	by Steve Evans, Flicker via Wikimedia Commons
	Fig. 11 – Kumkum	by Kadiv, Wikimedia Commons
	Fig. 12 – Kumkum	by Sarha & Iain, Flicker via Wikimedia Commons
14-15	Fig. 13 – Women's India Trust artisans, Mumbai	by Lynnea Bylund (own work)
15	Fig. 14 – Women's India Trust staff, Mumbai	by Lynnea Bylund (own work)
16	Fig. 15 – AVANI staff, students & founder Arun Chavin w/ Arun & Tushar Gandhi	by Lynnea Bylund (own work)
	Fig. 16 – Arun Gandhi, AVANI School, Kolhapur	by Lynnea Bylund (own work)
	Fig. 17 – Mother & Child, brickyards camp, Kolhapur	by Matt Rhoades (own work)
	Fig. 18 – AVANI students, Kolhapur	by Scott Kafora (own work)
17	Fig. 19 – AVANI Director Anuradha Bhosale	by Scott Kafora (own work)
	Fig. 20 – Anuradha Bhosale with rescued students	by Scott Kafora (own work)

IMAGE CREDITS (2 of 7)

PAGE	DESCRIPTION & SOURCE
18	Fig. 21 – AVANI students in recess, Kolhapur	by Lynnea Bylund (own work)
	Fig. 22 – Anuradha Bhosale with student, Kolhapur	by Matt Rhoades (own work)
	Fig. 23 – CRC/Women of Kolhapur	by Lynnea Bylund (own work)
19	Fig. 24 – AVANI rescue student, Sonali	by Lynnea Bylund (own work)
20	Fig. 25 – Aga Khan Palace, Pune	by DJOH.net (own work), Wikimedia Commons
	Fig. 26 – Aga Khan Palace, Pune	by Mat Fuller (own work)
	Fig. 27 – Informative Entry Plaque, Aga Khan Palace, Pune	Lynnea Bylund (own work)
	Fig. 28 – Aga Khan Palace, Pune	by Gaurav Yawalkar-Gade (own work), Wikimedia Commons
21	Fig. 29 – Mr. & Mrs. Gandhi, Aga Khan Palace, Pune	by Lynnea Bylund (own work)
22	'GOD IS EVERYWHERE' portrait at the Palace by Lynnea Bylund (own work)
	Bust of Kasturba Gandhi at Aga Khan Palace	by Lynnea Bylund (own work)
23	Great Sage Vivekananda greets all who enter Mumbai (+memorial plaque)	Lynnea Bylund (own work)
24	Fig. 30 – Skilled artisan of MarketPlace	SHARE, Old Mumbai	by Mat Fuller (own work)
	Fig. 31 – Happy child outside MarketPlace	SHARE, Old Mumbai	by Lynnea Bylund (own work)
	Fig. 32 – Hopeful vendor outside MarketPlace	SHARE, Old Mumbai	by Lynnea Bylund (own work)
	Fig. 33 – Devastating Monsoon of 2009, Mumbai	by Lakun Patra M.I.B., Wikimedia Commons
25	Fig. 34 – Artisan fabric loom, MarketPlace	SHARE	by Matthew T Rader (own work), Wikimedia Commons
26	Kasturba Gandhi 1915	Public Domain, Wikimedia Commons
	Gandhi leading the Salt March protest, 1930	Public Domain, Wikimedia Commons
	Gandhi deboarding at Old Ahmedabad Station		Public Domain, Wikimedia Commons
27	Fig. 35 – Gandhi exits a train in 'Bombay'	Public Domain, Wikimedia Commons
	Fig. 36 – The Mahatma receives a donation	Public Domain, Wikimedia Commons
28	Salt worker of the Little Rann desert	Mat Fuller (own work)
29	Fig. 37 – Traditional turbaned Kutch villager	by Kasturi Gandhi / Nipun Prabhakar (own work)
	Fig. 38 – Domesticated camel with village woman	by Kasturi Gandhi / Nipun Prabhakar (own work)
	Fig. 39 – Kutch villager tends to his goats	by Kasturi Gandhi / Nipun Prabhakar (own work)
30	Fig. 34 – The distinctly round 'Bhunga' homes of the Kutch	by Kasturi Gandhi / Nipun Prabhakar (own work)
	Fig. 35 – Inside a villager's 'Bhunga'	by Kasturi Gandhi / Nipun Prabhakar (own work)

IMAGE CREDITS

PAGE	DESCRIPTION & SOURCE
31	Fig. 36 – Exquisite leather shoecraft of the Kutch	by Kasturi Gandhi / Nipun Prabhakar (own work)
32	Fig. 37 – Hunnarshala artisan weaving a traditional 'charpai' (bed), Kutch	by Lynnea Bylund (own work)
	Fig. 38 – Hunnarshala artisan weaving a traditional 'charpai' (bed), Kutch	by Lynnea Bylund (own work)
	Fig. 39 – Hunnarshala artisan weaving a traditional 'charpai' (bed), Kutch	by Lynnea Bylund (own work)
33	Fig. 40 – Hunnarshala-built home with open kitchen, Bhuj Kutch	by Lynnea Bylund (own work)
	Fig. 41 – Distinct Kutch/ Hunnarshala roof/ceiling allowing daylight in	by Lynnea Bylund (own work)
	Fig. 42 – Hunnarshala experimental design concepts are ongoing	by Lynnea Bylund (own work)
	Fig. 43 – Hunnarshala design Kutch jeet-thatched roof/ceiling	by Lynnea Bylund (own work)
34	Fig. 44 – Hunnarshala rebuilt this neighborhood	by Hunnarshala Foundation, www. Hunnarshala.org
	Fig. 45 – Happy new Hunnarshala homeowner	by Hunnarshala Foundation, www. Hunnarshala.org
	Fig. 46 – Hunnarshala builder crew	by Hunnarshala Foundation, www. Hunnarshala.org
35	Fig. 47 – Kutch-style clay pottery	by Lynnea Bylund (own work)
	Fig. 48 – Weaving jeet in the Kutch	by Lynnea Bylund (own work)
	Fig. 49 – Jeet being dyed	by Lynnea Bylund (own work)
36	Fig. 50 – Drying the dyed jeet prior to weaving	by Lynnea Bylund (own work)
	Fig. 51 – Jeet dyed and ready for weaving	by Lynnea Bylund (own work)
	Fig. 52 – Clay water pot held in jeet macramé	by Lynnea Bylund (own work)
	Fig. 53 – Wall mural of traditional attire Kutch wife	by Lynnea Bylund (own work)
37	Fig. 54 – Crystal plucked from a dried salt marsh, Little Rann Kutch	by Lynnea Bylund (own work)
	Fig. 55 – Sunset over salt beds of the Rann	by Abu Sufian Mohammad, CreativeCommons.org
38-39	Fig. 56 – Father & son salt workers	by Lynnea Bylund (own work)
	Fig. 57 – Salt worker living quarters	by Lynnea Bylund (own work)
	Fig. 58 – Endless salt brings endless toil	by Vinod Panicker, Wikimedia Commons
	Fig. 59 – Motorcycle and owner in Little Rann	Mat Fuller (own work)
	Fig. 60 – Hard cracked ground of the summer Rann	by Lynnea Bylund (own work)

IMAGE CREDITS (4 of 7)

PAGE	DESCRIPTION & SOURCE
40	Fig. 61 – Iconic entrance to Gujarat Vidyapith	by Gazal World, Wikimedia
	Fig, 62 – Arun Gandhi mounting a power-generator cycle	by Lynnea Bylund (own work)
	Fig. 64 – India PM Nehru visits Gujarat Vidyapith in 1949	Public Domain via Wikimedia Commons
41	Fig. 65 – Mural of Gandhi's signature 'charkha' (spinning wheel)	by Lynnea Bylund (own work)
	Fig. 66 – Classroom for modern cotton-spinning technology	by Lynnea Bylund (own work)
42	Fig. 67 – Students mingle on campus	by Lynnea Bylund (own work)
	Fig. 68 – Wall mural depicts equality of religions	by Lynnea Bylund (own work)
	Fig. 69 – Students attend a Q&A with Legacy Tour delegates	by Lynnea Bylund (own work)
43	Fig. 70 – Sabarmati entry plaque	by Lynnea Bylund (own work)
	Fig. 71 – Gandhi's private quarters at Sabarmati Ashram	by Lynnea Bylund (own work)
44	Fig. 72 – Ashram where Gandhi lived 1917-30	by Lampurav, Wikimedia Commons
	Fig. 73 – Gandhi's bust adorns the Sabarmati grounds	by Hardik Jadeja, Wikimedia Commons
	Fig. 74 – Arun Gandhi, Sabarmati Ashram	by Lynnea Bylund (own work)
	Fig. 75 – Happy child at the Ashram entrance	by Lynnea Bylund (own work)
	Fig. 76 – Ganesh statue tends to Sabarmati garden	by Lynnea Bylund (own work)
45	Fig. 77 – Tushar Gandhi art hangs at Sabarmati	by Lynnea Bylund (own work)
	Fig. 78 – Arun gives Gandhi's 'charkha' a spin	by Lynnea Bylund (own work)
	Fig. 79 – Ashram Museum entrance sign	by Lynnea Bylund (own work)
	Fig. 80 – Gandhi greets all	by Lynnea Bylund (derivative from Helfman, Wikimedia Commons)
46	Fig. 81 – Three weary travelers, Tushar Gandhi w/ Lynnea & Arun	by Lynnea Bylund (own work)
	Fig. 83 – Sandals and glasses of the Mahatma	by K. Vishnupranay, Wikimedia Commons
46-47	Fig. 82 – Gandhi portrait leading Dandi Salt March	by Susant Purohit, Wikimedia Commons
	Fig. 84 – Gandhi's Prayer memorialized at Sabarmati	by Lynnea Bylund (own work)

IMAGE CREDITS (5 of 7)

PAGE	DESCRIPTION & SOURCE
48	Fig. 85 – 'Holy Cow' Ox in Ganeshpura	by Lynnea Bylund (own work)
49	Fig. 86 – SEWA ladies of Ganeshpura great Legacy Tour with lunch	by Lynnea Bylund (own work)
	Fig. 87 – SEWA ladies of Ganeshpura great Legacy Tour with lunch	by Lynnea Bylund (own work)
50	Fig. 88 – SEWA founder Ela Bhatt inspects a day's output	by T. Elders, Wikimedia Commons
	Fig. 89 – Skilled S.E.W.A. artisans work a design	by Lynnea Bylund (own work)
51	Fig. 90 – Ela Bhatt & followers cheer the ratification of SEWA 1972	Public Domain, Wikimedia Commons
	Fig. 91 – SEWA founder Ela Bhatt	by Mohan Juneja, Wikimedia Commons
52	Fig. 92 – SEWA Cooperative Bank & H.Q.	by Lynnea Bylund (own work)
53	Fig. 93 – Friendly inquisitive young people, Old Ahmedabad	Mat Fuller (own work)
	Fig. 94 – Elephant carries a hopeful vendor to market	by Lynnea Bylund (own work)
54	Fig. 95 – Shri Swaminarayan Temple, Old Heritage Walk	derivative by Lynnea Bylund (under ADMAX license)
	Fig. 96 – Hutheesing Jain Temple, Old Heritage Walk	derivative by Lynnea Bylund (under ADMAX license)
	Fig. 97 – Old Ahmedabad Heritage Walk	by Mat Fuller (own work)
55	Fig. 98 – Chatbutro bird hutch, Old Ahmedabad Heritage Walk	Nizil Shah, Wikimedia Commons
	Fig. 99 – Historic temple (B&W), Old Ahmedabad Heritage Walk	by Mat Fuller (own work)
	Fig. 100 – Shree Swaminarayan Temple Gateway	by Lynnea Bylund (own work)
56	Fig. 101 – Barefoot College direction sign, circa 1980	by Lynnea Bylund (own work)
56-57	Fig. 102 – Barefoot College solar class	by Pradeep Gaurs (under ADMAX license)
58	Fig. 103 – Solar Mama of Barefoot College with solar reflector	by Lynnea Bylund (own work)
	Fig. 104 – Barefoot students with newly built solar reflector	by Pradeep Gaurs (under ADMAX license)
	Fig. 105 – Solar Mamas reflected in solar dish mirrors	by Mat Fuller (own work)
59	Bunker Roy giving a Ted Talk	by Ashish Sunil Sahuji, Wikimedia Commons
60	Fig. 106 – Electric circuitry students of Barefoot College	by Lynnea Bylund (own work)
	Fig. 107 – Arun Gandhi with Bunker Roy in Tilonia Ajmer	by Mat Rhoades (own work)

IMAGE CREDITS (6 of 7)

PAGE	DESCRIPTION & SOURCE
61	Friendly marketplace vendor selling green onions	Mat Fuller (own work)
62-63	Fig. 108 - Tushar & Arun Gandhi w/ Waterman join at a newly dug 'johad dam'	by Lynnea Bylund (own work)
64	Fig. 109 – Design rendering of Johad	by Tarun Bharat Sangh (own work), visit www.TarunBharatSangh.in
	Fig. 110 – Brick and mortar reinforced Johad	by Birla Einstein, Wikimedia Commons
	Fig. 111 – Waterman sharing water wisdom	by Lynnea Bylund (own work)
	Fig. 112 – Johad amidst greenery where once was only dry desert	by Lynnea Bylund (own work)
65	Fig. 113 – Rajendra Singh, the Waterman of India	by Lynnea Bylund (own work)
66	Fig. 114 – Oxen plow Navdanya Farm fields	by Jacob Avanzato under ADMAX license)
67	Fig. 115 – Vandana points to the third-eye	by Lynnea Bylund (own work)
	Fig. 116 – Dr. Shiva at Voices Against Poverty, Berlin	by Matthias Muehlbradt, Wikimedia Commons
68	Fig. 117 – Dr. Shiva is gifted Beloved Adi Da's 'Not Two Is Peace'	by Lynnea Bylund (own work)
	Fig. 118 – Vandana Shiva with a sampling of Navdanya's seedbank	visit www.FriendsOfNavdanya.org
69	Fig. 119 – Sad newspaper headline January 30, 1948	Public Domain, Wikimedia Commons
70-71	Fig. 120 – World Peace Gong at Old Birla House	by Lynnea Bylund (own work)
	Fig. 121 – Old Birla House & Gandhi Smriti	by Adam Jones, Kelowna, BC, Wikimedia Commons
	Fig. 122 – Memoriam Einstein Prayer Garden rock inscription	by Adam Jones, BC, Wikimedia Commons
72	Fig. 123 – Prayer Garden path plaque	by Lynnea Bylund (own work)
	Fig. 124 – Gandhi's final footsteps	by Matt Stabile, Wikimedia Commons
	Fig. 125 – Flowers adorn Gandhi's footsteps and Samadhi site	by Fowler & Fowler, Wikimedia Commons
	Fig. 126 – Birla Red Urn at Eternal Gandhi Multimedia, Gandhi Smriti	by Saad Akhtar, Wikimedia Commons
73	Fig, 127 – Raj Ghat, Gandhi Cremation memorial grounds	by हिंदुस्थान वासी, Wikimedia Commons
	Figs. 128, 129, 130 – Cremation site components	by Lynnea Bylund (own work)
74	Fig. 131 – Raj Ghat cremation memorial	Humayunn Niaz Ahmed Peerzaada, Wikimedia Commons
75	Figs. 132, 133, 134 – Historic final stops	by Lynnea Bylund (derivatives of vintage public domain)
76	Fig. 135 – Qutub Minar reaching for the sky	by Mitulshekhaliya111, Wikimedia Commons
	Fig. 136 – Qutub Minar massive base	by Lynnea Bylund (own work)
	Fig. 138 – Alok Tiwari presents hand-carved stones adorning the Qutub Minar base	by Lynnea Bylund (own work)

IMAGE CREDITS

PAGE	DESCRIPTION & SOURCE
77	Fig. 137 – Sunset through an Islamic arch	by Lynnea Bylund (own work)
	Fig. 139 – Hindu deity escaped defacing by the Islamic builders	by Lynnea Bylund (own work)
	Fig. 140 – One of 5 tombs at Qutub Minar	by Lynnea Bylund (own work)
	Fig. 141 – Entrance to one of the tombs	by Lynnea Bylund (own work)
78-79	Fig. 142 – Taj Mahal on a glorious cloudless day	Joel Godwin, (own work) Creative Commons
80	Figs. 143, 144, 145 – Three views of the west-facing Taj mosque	by Lynnea Bylund (own work)
81	Fig. 146 – Tombs of Shah Jahan & Mumtaz Mahal	by W. Donelson, Taj-Mahal.net (Wikimedia Commons)
	Fig. 147 – Ganesh of Marble with jeweled inlay	by Lynnea Bylund (own work)
	Fig. 148 – Taj Mahal view with minaret	by Udayadittya, Wikimedia Commons
	Fig. 149 – Shah Jahan portrait, artist unknown	by Geking54k, Wikimedia Commons
82-83	Fig. 150 – Striking view of Agra Fort	by Rupeshsarkar (own work), Wikimedia Commons
83	Fig. 151 – Taj Mahal view from Agra Fort Shah Burj veranda	by A Ghosh 2020, Wikimedia Commons
84	Fig. 152 – Morning up-close view of Agra Fort	by Ishita Gupta, Wikimedia Commons
	Fig. 153 – Panorama of Agra Fort on a cloudless day	by DeepSheel09, Wikimedia Commons
85	Fig. 154 – Smiling Goddess sculpture at Indira Gandhi Int'l	by Debashishalder13, Wikimedia Commons
86-87	Fig. 155 – Imposing beautiful elephants sculpture at Delhi Airport	by TechnoAyan, Wikimedia Commons
87	Fig. 156 – Artistic display of Namaskara Sun Salute Yoga	by Jnanaranjan Sahu, Wikimedia Commons
88	Fig. 157 – Handwritten message at Sabarmati	by Lynnea Bylund (derivative of Vijay Barot, Wikimedia Commons)
89	Epilogue 'Gandhi's Talisman of Recall'	by Lynnea Bylund (own work)
90	Fig. 158 – AVANI School Eco Dome, Kolhapur	by Lynnea Bylund (own work)
	Fig. 159 – AVANI Class Sand Art For Peace	by Lynnea Bylund (own work)
	Fig. 160 – Frances Bylund assists an elder along Old Ahmedabad 'Heritage Walk'	by Lynnea Bylund (own work)
91	Wild peacock in the countryside near Mumbai	by Lynnea Bylund (derivative work under ADMAX license)
102	Legacy Group & Guides at Navdanya Farm 2010 during Kumbha Mela	by Lynnea Bylund (own work)
	Legacy Travelers January 2018, Birla House Peace Gong	by Tushar Gandhi (own work)
106	Blessed by a child in Kolhapur	by Scott Kafora (own work)
107	Lynnea Bylund at Navdanya Farm, Dehradun, 2010 Kumbha Mela Pilgrimage	Scott Kafora (own work)
108	Not-Two Is Peace', Adi Da Samraj	visit www.Da-Peace.com
BACK COVER	Legacy Travelers January 2018, Birla House Peace Gong	by Tushar Gandhi (own work)

PRAISE FOR GANDHI LEGACY TOUR

The Gandhi Legacy Tour of India was life-changing. As an American working on behalf of nonviolence, I gained new depth, connection and vitality for carrying the Mahatma's work into future generations.

Kit Miller
Director Emeritus
M.K. Gandhi Institute for Nonviolence

To say that the Gandhi Legacy Tour proved to be a timely change agent in my life is such a poor attempt to express the ongoing impact of the living imprint of a man whose Spirit remains alive and vital in the evolution of human history.

Hal Edwards
Pastor
Wauconda, Illinois

Traveling through India with Dr. Arun Gandhi, visiting the places where Bapuji lived, worked and influenced many millions of people, brings his work to life. It's a personal highlight that has impacted how I live and work as well as those of my students

Dr. Brian Polkinghorn
Professor of Conflict Resolution
Salisbury University

The Gandhi Legacy Tour in India awakened a deep sense of purpose in me. Arun leads a masterful exploration into the heart of Gandhiji's blossoming legacy on this extraordinary journey. The wisdom of Gandhiji's experiments in truth are as relevant as ever, and continually inspires great clarity in me.

Shelley Fritz
Graduate Student
Kansas State University

We met Arun Gandhi at a book signing and learned about the Gandhi Legacy Tour. Mahatma Gandhi has had such an impact on my life, and after meeting Arun, I knew this tour would help our magazine become a platform for changemakers around the world, furthering the legacy of Gandhi's philosophy of nonviolence and peace!

Missy Crutchfield
Co-Founder, Gandhi's Be Magazine
& Gandhi Global Center for Peace

The Gandhi Legacy Tour was one of the most impactful experiences of my life. Every aspect of t his tour is educational, from the amazing organizations visited, to seeing the historic sites in Gandhi's life, to the stories that Arun Gandhi tells about living with his grandfather. Arun's Legacy Tour truly brings his grandfather's legacy alive with his tireless work for a more peaceful and just world.

Dr. Margaret McLaren
Professor of Philosophy
Rollins College

My time in India with Gandhi grandson and great grandson, Arun & Tushar Gandhi, changed my life forever. From the physical exploration of villages, ashrams, palaces, earthen dome homes, and the Taj Mahal, to the spiritual discoveries of sustainability, and 'The 6 Stepping Stones of Gandhian Philosophy' my father and I were forever transformed.

Tony Scruggs
Actor & Empathy Coach
Former Major League Baseball Player

GANDHI LEGACY TOUR OF INDIA TRAVELERS
(1999 to 2018)

Led by Arun, Sunanda, and Tushar Gandhi
India Travel Partner – Travel Passion
India Tour Guide – Alok Tiwari

Melissa Toft	Molly Vicerra	Ruth Sheldon	Schera Chadwick
Constanze Frank	Lynn Classen	Mavis Aldridge	Ed Lollis
Katherine N. Miller	Sandra Vierck	John Lombard	Yvonne LeGear
Roger Charles Newman	Victor Vinkey	Thomas Lyle	Judy White
Janet Wall	Sean Bray	Beth Barry	Catherine Torpey
Victor Kazanjian	Deborah Sublett	Dyann Pettigrew	Paule Pfeifer
Carrie Trybulec	Danny Sublett	Betty Edwards	Tina Marie Arnold
Kevin Walke	Barbara Carlisle	Martha Sarkissian	William Stone
Audre Wiksell Newman	Robert Brown	Marty McCall	Antonio Canseco
Richard Tolliver	Margaret Fleming	Pilar Laso	Leslie Roth
Janet Traxler	Joe Fleming II	Vicki Brooks	Joan Bragen
Amy Foster	Larry Johnson	Jane Martin	Tracey Lake
Jeanette Ben Farhat	Sally Johnson	Leah Pransky	Jennifer Nelson
Anna-Helena Iennaco	Jose Zarate	Joan Pransky	Sarah Schmidt
Jeanne Hahn	Colin Crossey	Leslie Roth	Megan Nicely
Reed Holt	Kendall Burner	Meghan Roth	James Forman
Rosemary Holt	Dawn Pisturino	Patricia Mulloy	Ifeoma Nwokoye
Jayne Brechwald	Johanna Plaut	Mary Mulloy	John Corbett
Gary Elkins	Thomas Plaut	David John Pelle	Norma Green
Lee Cockerill	Carl Doerner	Ruth Cascone	Diane Pearson
Joan Cockerill	Alex Sardar	Sarah Presley	Alvaro Arellano
Frances Catelon-McIntire	Jack Vahan Bournazian	David Schecter	Vicky Rossi
Sandy Kaiser	Audrey Geis	Harriet Rohmer	Bascom Talley
Roger Kaiser	Patricia Hewitt	Marianne Milloy	Sami Awa
Richard Tolliver	Andrianna Dafnis	Margaret McLaren	Alycia Dasmann
June Brashares	Karen Schlumpp	Todd Menzing	Tera Hoffman
Tomoko Takeda	Joseph Hummel	Karen Harris	Mario Sacasa
Shelmin Hassanali	Robert Daniels	Shannon Babcock	Cynthia Ideker
James Turo	Marie Erikson	Tanya Phillips	Ken Preston-Pile
Marcia Meyers	Andrea Buffa	Jill Appel	Julio Valdes
Beverly Burlett	Ellie Adelman	Barbara Washington-Grant	Molly (Monica) Marsh
Rose Aguilar	David Csizmadia	Darren Hamm	Shirley Hess
Arnold Panitch	Janet Chilsom	Johanna Hamm	Jill Schultz

> "I have watched the cultures of all lands blow around my house and other winds have blown the seeds of peace, for travel is truly the language of peace." – Gandhi

Randon Ryland
Patrick Robbins
Walter Muelken
Barbara Briggs-Letson
Bruce Baumgartner
Hal Edwards
William Ruppert
Dorothy Ruppert
Valerie Warren
Araceli Campos
Diana Moore
Barbara McDonald
Carolyn Jerard
Elizabeth Robertson
Ines Johanson
Josaphine Showalter
Navid Ardakani
Miriam Calabro
Jerry T. Lawler
Maureen Powers
Paul Etchemendy
Dorothy Abbott
Anish Prasad
Kristin Lynn Kumpf
Kelle Marie Rose
Joel Langdon
Sally Kay Lindsey
Frances Drake
Hazel Roberta Bond
Linda Whitmyre

Polly Connelly
Zoe Nelson Bidell
Kai Benjamin Nelson Bidell
Thomas Richard Bidell
Charlotte O'Kelly
Larry Carney
David Litwak
Teegrey Iannuzzi
Barbara Gerten
Jennifer Ann Nelson
John Richard Whelehan
Cassandra Abbe Downs
Cynthia Lou Medina
Lori Agnes Smith
Jo Ann Kudlek
Joseph Antony Calcaterra
Janet Ruth Calcaterra
Brenda Macauley
Felicity Davis
Pieter Stathis
Kathryn Kerch Smith
Garth Dyke
Tara Mulvey
Ranjan Kamath
Natalia Grossman
Joanna Amaral
Jean Templeton Williams
Scott Franklin Kafora
Archana Prasad
Alison Venuti Engels

Marc Raymond Scruggs
Anthony Raymond Scruggs
Judith Kahn
Lynnea Bylund
Paul A. Sartori
Alison Venuti Engels (2x)
Maria Engels
August Lorwood
Rebecca Johnson
Bill Destler
Elizabeth Bobo
Gaylinn Greenwood
Gerald Lee Brown
Kathleen Sbarbaro
Meridel Phillips
Nick Grau
Robert Grau
Shari Zaret
Shelley Fritz
Stephanie Brown
Susan Kochan
Abigail Kochan
Zach Kochan
Mathew Rhoades
Charles Almer
David Lange
Lauren McMillion
William John Barron III
Rosemary Touyanou
Shannon Richmond

Lois E. Coleman
Monica Hegnerlynn
Donna Jo Koechig
Missy Crutchfield
Susan K. Talley
The Refugee Response (3)
Gaylea Prichard-Silvers
Karline McLain
Sarah Rose Cukier
Tatiana Roe
Mary Bethany Vincent
Nicole McGee
Cassandra Curley
Alexandria J. Tomkunas
Rachel A. Wasserman
Jennifer Sands
Lynnea Bylund (2x)
Martha DeWolf Kirby
Victoria Burg
Thomas Cook
Mat Fuller
Courtney Fuller
Margaret McLaren (2x)
LaToya Dunbar
Persha Carlston
Melinda Caparco
Cindy Rice
Sheila Y. Cantrell
Frances E. Bylund

(Gandhi Legacy Tour of India has generated over $1,000,000 in philanthropic tourism revenues and donations)

Legacy Travelers, Jan 2010 (Navdanya Farm) & Jan 2017 (Birla House Peace Gong)

THE SEVEN SOCIAL SINS

Politics without principles

Wealth without work

Pleasure without conscience

Knowledge without character

Commerce without morality

Science without humanity

Worship without sacrifice

~ M.K. Gandhi

M.K. GANDHI AND TEA

Mahatma Gandhi wrote in his book found online 'A Key to Health' why tannin, the compound that gives tea its astringency, was bad for human consumption. Previous to that Gandhi liked to drink tea throughout the day, at least until a journalist interviewing him remarked, "Mr. Gandhi it seems that you cannot be without this stimulant, tea!" Gandhi thought for a while and from that day forward he gave up drinking the conventional black tea; and he instead opted for a simple beverage of lemon, ginger and honey, said to this day to enhance stomach, heart, liver, and skin health.

GRANDFATHER GANDHI'S TEA RECIPE
by Arun Gandhi

It is a very simple concentrate

Fresh or organic lemon juice (48 oz)
Two heaping teaspoons of ginger paste
Mix ginger paste into juice of lemon
Add one-half teaspoon of salt
and give it a good shake

When you want a cup of tea just
take two to three tablespoons
of the mixture in a mug full of hot
water and add honey to taste.

ABOUT THE GANDHI LEGACY TOURS

The Gandhi Legacy Tours are unusual in that they do not focus on places of tourist interest but places of human interest. The tours are designed to educate participants in the essence of Gandhi's philosophy of nonviolence, and how individuals can apply it in their own lives to bring about socio-economic change. Since 1999 Arun Gandhi has brought his grandfather's philosophy of nonviolence to westerners. The focus is on studying institutions that apply the philosophy of nonviolence in their attempt to transform communities, in both urban and rural areas. Gandhi believed in creating a "Sarvodaya" society - a society where everyone would enjoy a reasonable standard of living with attendant rights and privileges, and the Legacy Tours demonstrate that humble "change-makers" are "being the change" and manifesting a Sarvodaya reality.

ABOUT DR. ARUN GANDHI

Born in 1934 in Durban, South Africa, Arun Gandhi is the fifth grandson of Mohandas K. "Mahatma" Gandhi. Growing up under the discriminatory apartheid laws of South Africa, he was beaten by "white" South Africans for being too black, and "black" South Africans for being too white. However, he learned from his parents and grandparents that justice does not mean revenge, it means transforming the opponent through love and suffering. Having spent nearly two years with his Grandfather Arun learned to understand nonviolence through understanding violence. "If we know how much passive violence we perpetrate against one another we will understand why there is so much physical violence plaguing societies and the world today," the Mahatma told Arun. For the past decade, Arun has participated in the Renaissance Weekend deliberations with President Clinton and other well-respected Rhodes Scholars. Arun shares the lessons he learned from this grandfather with audiences all over the world.

ABOUT DR. TUSHAR GANDHI

In 1996 Tushar Gandhi, son of Arun Gandhi and co-leader of the Gandhi Legacy Tours, was appointed President of the Lok Seva Trust, a voluntary organization working for the economically weaker sections of Mumbai. He established the Mahatma Gandhi Foundation to make Gandhi's message available globally on the Internet. Tushar was also invited to join the Advisory Committee on Cyber Crime. He was appointed by the Prime Minister of India to the subcommittee of the Gandhi Smriti and Darshan Samiti (Gandhi National Museum). Tushar is involved with the US based peace organization 'Seeds for Peace' which works with children from troubled areas of the world. In 2005, to mark the 75th Anniversary of the 1930 Salt March, Tushar organized a 241-mile walk for Peace, Justice and Freedom along with 600 marchers from India, Pakistan, the US, UK and other parts of the world. The Mahatma Gandhi Foundation was awarded the 1st 'Mahatma Mahaveer Award' for promoting Gandhian ideals. Tushar is the author of Let's Kill Gandhi: A definitive study of the Hindu Fundamentalist plot to assassinate Gandhi.

Throughout our journey across India we were met with the traditional Hindu greeting of 'Namasté' – a word derived from Sanskrit that means "the divine oneness in me bows to the divine oneness in you."

Namasté represents the idea that all are one divine consciousness in prior unity. It affirms that beneath the outer trappings that make us appear different from one another, we are made of the same stuff – we are more the same than we are different.

MEET THE AUTHOR …

Lynnea Bylund is the former Managing Director of Gandhi Legacy Tours, Director Emeritus of Gandhi Worldwide Education Institute, and Founder of Catalyst House; and has over three decades of experience in corporate administration, marketing and business development. Through the 90s she was a nationally recognized spokeswoman for emerging broadband video and information delivery industries.

Lynnea has a degree in holistic health and nutrition from the legendary and controversial health researcher, educator and activist Doctor Kurt Donsbach; and she is the author of the well-received, "Health IS Wealth," a DIY guide to attaining optimal health using essential holistic principles.

She is the founder of two not-for-profit small business-based wireless trade associations and has lobbied on Capitol Hill and at the FCC where she has spoken out strongly against the cable TV monopoly, illegal spectrum warehousing and ill-conceived congressional schemes to auction our nation's airwaves to the highest bidder.

In 1995 Lynnea became the first female in the world to be awarded a Broadband PCS operating permit – she was one of only 18 winners, along with Sprint, AT&T, and Verizon, in the biggest cash auction in world history - raising a whopping $7.7 billion. In the mid-90s Lynnea also led the successful development and historic launch of the first commercial cable TV systems in the South Pacific Island Nations.

Lynnea at Navdanya Farm, 2010 Kumbha Mela Pilgrimage

FOLLOW LYNNEA & CATALYST HOUSE –

Twitter.com/lynneabylund | Linkedin.com/in/catalysthouse
Pinterest.com/catalysthouse/pins | Youtube.com/catalysthouse/videos
GandhiForChildren.org | GandhiTour.info | LynneaBylund.com

MORE INFO -or- DONATIONS
For more information, or to make or consider your gracious donation to any of the groups featured in Gandhi Legacy Tour, a list of organizations' links is maintained for your convenience at our website.
www.CatalystHouse.net/donations

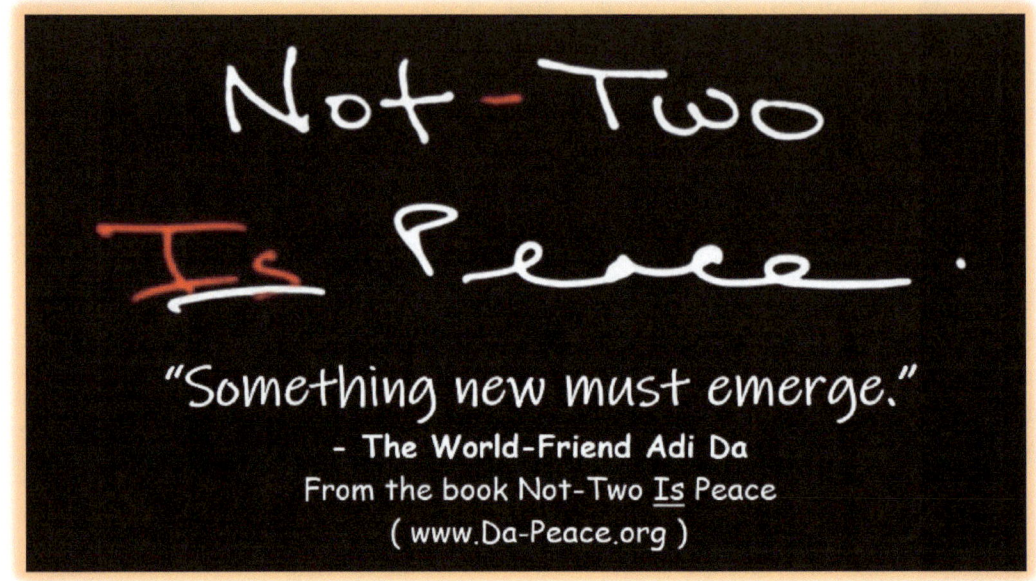

VISIT
www.Da-Peace.org

www.ingramcontent.com/pod-product-compliance
Lightning Source LLC
Chambersburg PA
CBHW041533220426
43662CB00002B/43